A

## OTHER TITLES BY THE SAME AUTHOR

### *Other novels by the same author*
OF MASKS AND MINDS
LAWS BE THEIR ENEMY
LYDIA TRENDENNIS
THE SIN AND THE SINNERS
THE GROTTO OF TIBERIUS
THE DEVIL BEHIND ME
THE STORM KNIGHT
WATERLOO (In conjunction with the Dino de Laurentiis film)
THE WIDER SEA OF LOVE
THE WAR GOD
A KILLING FOR THE HAWKS (Mark Twain Literary Award)
THE TORMENTED
THE OBSESSION
THE MYSTERIOUS AFFAIR

### *Novels in the same series:*
RAGE OF THE INNOCENT
IN PRESENCE OF MY FOES
YEARS OF THE FURY

633 SQUADRON
633 SQUADRON: OPERATION RHINE MAIDEN
633 SQUADRON: OPERATION CRUCIBLE
633 SQUADRON: OPERATION VALKYRIE
633 SQUADRON: OPERATION COBRA
633 SQUADRON: OPERATION TITAN
633 SQUADRON: OPERATION CRISIS
633 SQUADRON: OPERATION THOR
633 SQUADRON: OPERATION DEFIANT
633 SQUADRON: OPERATION SAFEGUARD

SAFFRON'S WAR
SAFFRON'S ARMY
SAFFRON'S TRIALS

A MEETING OF STARS
A CLASH OF STARS

THE PERSUADERS
Books 1, 2 and 3 from the TV series of the same name

*Novels under the pseudonym of DAVID FARRELL*
TEMPTATION ISLE
STRANGE ENEMY
VALLEY OF CONFLICT
THE OTHER COUSIN
TWO LOVES
MULLION ROCK

*Plays*
The Glass Prison
A House Divided

*Non-fiction*
WRITE A SUCCESSFUL NOVEL
(written in conjunction with Moe Sherrard-Smith)

A YOUTHFUL ABSURDITY
(Volume One of a three volume autobiography)

*Short Stories*
Over 80 short stories published
Short listed for Winston Churchill Fellowship
Short listed for CWA'S Golden Dagger Award

*Shelagh*

My tribute and dedication to my late wife,
**Shelagh**

## I MUST BELIEVE, MY LOVE

I must believe, my love
For you I must believe
That when this race is o'er and done,
My love and I will embrace again,
In a world secured of pain.

For if you were not there, my love,
With no hand to put in mine,
There would be no victory or acclaim,
I would have run my race in vain,
A sad and futile game.

And if I were not there for you, my love.
I would scream at my betrayal,
For love to me is a deathless thing
And surely God himself must know
'Tis wrong to kill a thing as pure as snow.

So I must believe, my love,
That in this world of deceit and crime,
One thing does rise and survive its time,
A love that glows and shines so bright,
It can burn its way through time and night.

So for you, my love, I must believe,
That God is there and keeps his claim
That love can conquer and banish pain,
So my wish, my love (nay my very creed)
That because of you I must believe.

# AN AUTHOR'S ABSURDITIES

An Autobiography: Volume 2

# Frederick E. Smith

*Emissary Publishing*
P.O. Box 33, Bicester, OX26 2BU, UK.
Tel: 01869 323447   www.emissary-publishing.com

First published in Great Britain 2012
by Emissary Publishing, P.O. Box 33, Bicester, OX26 2BU, UK.
www.emissary-publishing.com
www.frederick-e-smith.com

British Library Cataloguing-in-Publication Data.
A catalogue record for this book is available from the British Library.

ISBN: 978-1-874490-81-4

©Frederick E. Smith

SOURCES OF INFORMATION
My mother's autobiography
My father's notes
My own diaries, letter files, and memories

All rights reserved. This book may not be reproduced, in whole or in part, in any form (except by reviewers for the public press), without written permission from the publisher.

Printed and bound by MWL Print Group Ltd., South Wales.

# FOREWORD

There comes a time when a man feels the need to pay tribute to those who have nurtured, guided, and supported him throughout his life. My debt to them is immeasurable and I can only hope this autobiography and the one that precedes it does them justice.

However, events have a way of shaping a man's life too, and in chronicling them I have the hope, forlorn though it may be, that I might be better understood and even forgiven by those whose patience I must have tried so often.

This second volume of my memoirs has yet another purpose. In covering my fifty years as a novelist, it gives account of my many experiences with agents, film companies, editors and publishers. There may be some, novice writers in particular, who as yet respect or even admire the literary establishment and its many branches. There might even be those who still hold the belief that, along with the wine trade, publishing is one of the last resorts of the gentleman. In my time I was that naive myself.

For such people who know nothing of the injuries inflicted on authors by those who live and profit from their work, this volume might offer a surprise. Indeed, the laziness, inefficiency, and sometimes near criminal neglect described might be hard to believe did I not hold letters to prove every statement made. Because I love literature and want to see it better served by all the industries that profit from it, my personal traumas are told in the faint hope they might play some small part in that improvement.

At the same time, in recalling disappointments and injuries, I hope I have always retained my sense of humour. That is the one thing a writer must never allow them to pilfer or damage. It is his one lifeline to survival.

*My Mother,*
*(née* Elma Constance Escreet)

*My Father* (Harry Sydney Smith)

## ONE

My euphoria at returning home from the war with my full faculties and with the girl I loved waiting for me, came under threat the day after my return. Although I knew that four of my closest friends had survived the war, rumour reached me that Des Matthews had been shot down and killed that year.

As a result, when I phoned his home the following morning, I was prepared for the worst, and as I heard the phone being lifted, I was mentally rehearsing words of condolence. Instead, I heard a voice I knew so well. After adventures that would have filled a novel, Des was home and well, and his delight at hearing I was back matched my own. He was now engaged to the widow of his brother, who had been killed over Berlin earlier in the war. It all called for a celebration and we wasted no time in having one. That same night the four of us had dinner when the two girls met their fiancé's friend about whom they had heard so much.

It was a night to remember. We had years of emotion to release and a hundred experiences to relate. The wine flowed freely and the world had never seemed a richer or more rewarding place. I remember thinking again what a lucky man I was.

The following day Shelagh and I began our plans for marriage. The tiny house into which my parents had moved had only two bedrooms, and although my parents were sensible enough to allow Shelagh and I to share one, I was not unaware of the embarrassment they felt when neighbours, under the cloak of affability, asked how they were managing to 'cope' now that I was back and that sweet little girl from South Africa had arrived. It had taken more than a war with Hitler to destroy Northern Puritanism.

Not that Shelagh and I were driven into a hasty marriage. There was nothing we wanted more, particularly because of the uncertainty of my future. I could not forget the warning I had been given that I might be sent back to the Far East at any time. So with Frank Gosling and my father as witnesses, Shelagh and I were married in the local Registry Office on the 7th July 1945. The short service was read and I put the ring on Shelagh's finger. As we looked at one another, I think our thoughts were the same. For years and years it had seemed an impossible dream. Too many obstacles had lain in the way; too many forces beyond our control had kept us apart. Yet it had happened. We had met again and were now married. Dreams can come true after all.

I think for the rest of that day we were in a daze at the miracle of it. We hardly spoke. We just kept exchanging glances and holding hands as if to convince ourselves it was true. Our pent up emotions were to be discharged later.

We decided to spend our honeymoon in London. I think we both would have preferred the country but finances gave us little choice. My brother had offered us his flat, and because my savings had been stolen on the ship that had brought me back to England, we were extremely short of money.

*My brother, Raymond*

At this time, acutely conscious of the massive sacrifices Shelagh had made for me, I wanted to give her a wonderful honeymoon and

I remember feeling bitter about our penury. I was still smarting about the ship incident and my feelings were not helped by the Guildhall's reaction to my marriage.

Prior to the war, despite our poor salaries, we were always being asked to make contributions towards colleagues' marriages, and as the staff was large, gifts of bedroom suites and presents of even greater value were commonplace. For servicemen there were no such perks. Many of our colleagues were still in the Forces and because so many years had passed since our days there, the present staff did not know us. As a result, when Frank Gosling did the rounds for me, the sum total he received was ten pounds, and I suspect he contributed at least half that sum himself.

Nevertheless, some gesture had to be made, if only to placate my sense of frustration, and so I decided to travel down to London first class and to spend one night in a London hotel, whose name I have forgotten. After that we would come down to earth and spend the rest of the honeymoon in my brother's humble flat. The trip down to London stays in my memory for one reason.

Godfrey Winn, then a well-known novelist, shared our compartment with his agent. Although at that time I had little or no hope of becoming a professional writer, the wish must have been there because I unashamedly listened to their conversation and found myself envying the urbane Winn.

Our first night in London was not a success. It began auspiciously enough when Shelagh discovered one of the South African girls, who had travelled to England on the same ship as she, was staying in the hotel with the man she had crossed the ocean to marry, a Dutchman. We spent a couple of hours together and Shelagh seemed full of fun and gaiety. Yet when the others left our room, her mood changed and she began sobbing her heart out.

It was a miracle it had not happened before. As I knew only too well, before she had left South Africa to marry me her ex-husband had demanded his pound of flesh and insisted that her child, Barry, was handed over to him. What I had not appreciated was her astonishing courage and self-control which had enabled her to bottle up her anguish in order not to distress my parents. Now, freed at last from this need, her loss was exploding in a torrent of grief.

My shame was quite intense when I realized the massive effort she must have made during those weeks in Hull before and after my arrival. Selfishly, I had been so full of relief at my return, so happy at our reunion, that I had not given full consideration to the extent of her sacrifice. Perhaps it was because I had been so long away from South Africa that time had dulled my memory of her suffering there. Perhaps, even worse, I had thought about it but not allowed it to disturb the happiness I was enjoying.

Whatever the reasons, and I can't find excuses for any of them, I don't believe we had discussed it until this first night of our honeymoon. Now the pain she had hidden for two months was flooding out and I was quite shattered by its intensity.

Although I wanted above anything in the world to help her, I was acutely conscious my efforts were inadequate. They were too inhibited by the knowledge that, no matter how she tried through her tears to assure me she held me in no blame, I was still the man who had caused her all this suffering.

In short I believe I failed her that night and in the nights that followed. Part of my failure came from my own flawed temperament. When I feel guilt and can find no way of expurgating it, my mood can sometimes turn into frustration. At the very moment I desperately want to express my regret, I find myself saying things that only exacerbate the situation.

I fear that this happened during those few short days in London. I can only hope that when at last her tears dried, it was because her pain had run its course — at least for the moment — and was not due to a feeling that I was unsympathetic. The truth was I felt quite dreadful about it and went through agonies of self-recrimination.

Although minor ones in comparison, there were other factors that made our short honeymoon in London a failure. My brother's flat lay behind the huge Black Cat cigarette factory. Although its position had proved advantageous during the war because the towering factory had given the flat shelter from the VI rockets, it consisted of only one room, with a first floor landing toilet shared by all the other inhabitants in the building.

Neither of us would have cared about these primitive conditions under normal circumstances. But the tenants of the flat directly above seemed to hold a party every night, with the result that people were tramping down to the toilet every few minutes. In addition I was not yet rehabilitated. For a long time I had not known physical comforts, and I couldn't sleep in a soft bed. Moreover, I was finding London itself a great strain. With neither of us knowing the city well, the friend that Ray was staying with insisted on taking us to all London's well-known landmarks, and I was finding the crowded streets oppressive. I had never been at ease among crowds even when a boy, and my life style for many months could hardly have been more different. As a consequence, when the tramping feet from the upstairs flat and the constantly flushing toilet allowed me sleep, my dreams were full of hordes rushing at me and trampling me to death.

I think we endured it for four days. It was not all bad. Richard Tauber was conducting his operetta Old Chelsea and Ray obtained seats for us. That was the one outing we enjoyed. After it we thanked Ray for his kindness and fled from the city.

On our return from London, realizing the trip had been a failure, my father sent a telegram to Hannah and William in the Yorkshire village of Ruston Parva asking if we could stay with them. A reply came quickly. They would like nothing better; we must come at once.

We caught a bus the same day and were in Ruston Parva in the late afternoon. As I unlatched the garden gate, both of the old folk hurried out to greet us. William, in shirt sleeves and braces as always, gave me his gnarled hand and Hannah, as excited as a young girl, made a great fuss of Shelagh and told us that we would use their bedroom during our stay. When we protested, William gave his wicked wink and said the bed was the only one in the cottage fit for a honeymoon couple.

I knew the bedroom from my young days when my parents had slept there. It was full of heavy mahogany furniture, old prints, and had a huge brass double bed with a deep feather bed mattress. From the window one looked out across the pebbled lane to the fields where I had played as a child.

After the turmoil of London, it was like heaven to me. During the days we went for long walks or bicycle rides, took the bus to Bridlington, or played tennis in Driffield. In the evenings, after supper with the old folk, we would light the oil lamp in our room, and, in its mellow glow, sink into the billowing clouds of that superb bed and into each other's arms. In the mornings we would waken to the sound of a carrier's cart on the lane outside and soft country voices passing the time of the day. After all that had happened it was easy to imagine we had been transported into another and saner world.

Nor was it without its humour. The first time we cycled to Driffield to play tennis it was a fine, hot day and so Shelagh decided to go in her South African tennis shorts. As these reached up to the top of her thighs and English shorts still reached down to the knees, the effect on the locals was electric. With every person we passed on the four mile journey turning to stare at her open-mouthed, we laughed so much we were almost too tired to play tennis at the end of our ride.

*Shelagh, winner of The Grand Challenge Competition*

We returned to Hull ten days later, rested and refreshed, and ignorant of the alarms, discomforts, and misfortunes that were soon to descend on us. The first unpleasant news was carried in a military letter my father handed to me. It told me to report to Cranwell in two days time. Knowing we would be back before the deadline, my parents had kept the news from us.

My first fear was that the threatened Far Eastern posting had come though. If so, Cranwell would be the place to receive it. My memories of Cranwell, born in 1941, were of a huge soulless camp full of yelling, bullying MPs who operated in an ambience of gloom and freezing fog. Although I was no longer the rookie I had been then and it was summer, I still had forebodings when I said goodbye to Shelagh and my parents and took the train to Grantham.

At first, although I still found the camp oppressive, I was hugely relieved to be told nothing about an overseas posting and to find instead that I was to be in charge of the camp's skeet range where I would instruct would-be air gunners and observers. These seemed relatively congenial duties and, moreover, although I was given a billet with other veterans from the Far East, I was told that as a married man, I was eligible to live out of camp if I could find suitable accommodation.

Excited by this news, I rushed at my first opportunity into Sleaford, the nearest town, and began searching for a room or rooms so that Shelagh could come down and stay with me.

The search proved as difficult as everything else did at that time. With such a huge camp only seven miles away, it seemed every house was chock-a-block with married servicemen. After searching for a week, I was about to try further afield, when one of my men tipped me off that an overseas posting had left two rooms in Sleaford empty. Knowing they would be snapped up as swiftly as gold sovereigns from a plate, I got the address from him and was back in Sleaford within the hour.

The house was in London Road and owned by two elderly sisters, one a widow and the other a spinster. They were as sweet and delicate as old lace and, like their house, old fashioned in every way except for the rent they asked. This was so high that I doubted we could afford it without going hungry. But I wanted Shelagh with me so badly, I closed my eyes and accepted their terms.

She arrived a few days later. It was our first home together and it seemed like heaven in spite of our empty pockets. My diary records that when our money was laid out for the rent, the food, the bills, and essential bus fares, we could afford to go to the cinema once a month and I could have one pint of beer during the same period, and that was only in the NAAFI where beer was cheaper.

None of this mattered. We were young, we were together again, and it was still high summer. I borrowed a bicycle from a colleague to save the bus fares to and from the camp, and as our days ended at 5.30 unless we had some duty to perform I would arrive back in time for us to spend the long mellow evenings together.

We spent them walking down the country lanes or, if it rained, sitting together listening to the radio. I have only to hear Ivor Novello's song 'We'll Gather Lilacs' which was popular at that time, to remember those days. With all the stress and uncertainty that had gone before, they were as rich and golden as the summer sunlight itself and some of the happiest I have ever known.

Perhaps they were too good to last. We had not enjoyed them for more than two weeks before I received notice that I was being posted back to the Far East and to be ready by the end of the following week.

Although in some ways I was not surprised, it was a body blow. After five years abroad I had only been back in England for two months and to be sent back again so soon seemed inhumane.

Although my Section Officer was sympathetic, I received little more than a shrug from a Wing Commander who interviewed me. I was in the Armed Services and the war was anything but over. Moreover, there were not many SAIs in the Far East and I would be needed when the assault on Japan was made. That was the end of the affair.

I don't know what I would have done if Shelagh had not been in England. It is a hypothetical question to which I have no answer. But Shelagh was in England and because of me she had given up practically everything she had in the world to live in a strange country. Then how could I leave her stranded here for three more years with the additional possibility I might never return?

I could see no alternative but to fight the order and so asked to see the Station Welfare officer. He showed considerable sympathy when I put my case and advised me to seek medical advice. If a doctor decided Shelagh's mental or physical condition might deteriorate if I were posted overseas, there was a chance the order might be rescinded.

So I went back to Sleaford that night and told Shelagh what she must do. Never one to exaggerate any misfortune, medical or otherwise, she thought at first I was concerned about her health because of the way she had behaved in London. It was only when I told her about my posting that her protests died. Like myself, she could hardly believe I was to be sent back only a few weeks after my return.

So we made an appointment with a local doctor and I waited anxiously for the outcome. An hour later she returned home with a letter stating that she was suffering from hypertension and she should not be subjected to further worry and stress or her health might deteriorate further. Feeling more hopeful, I handed the letter to the Welfare Office the following morning and he promised to do all he could with it.

The weekend passed and three more anxious days followed. I was due to leave on the Friday for an overseas dispersal centre and when Wednesday arrived with no news, it looked as if our bid had failed. But in the afternoon my Section Officer called me to his office. Looking relieved, he told me my posting had been temporarily cancelled and I could return to my duties.

Our relief can be imagined. At the risk of sliding into debt, we even raided our piggy bank and treated ourselves to a night at the cinema. At the same time, neither of us forgot that word 'temporarily' and the shadow of it lay over us in the weeks that followed.

## TWO

Greatly relieved by my escape, I plunged into my duties with more enthusiasm. Given four fitters to work with me, I designed shelters for my clay pigeon traps and had them built in a field well away from the main camp. My task when they were finished was to show the Cranwell College students how to use a 12 bore shotgun and how to hit swiftly-moving targets. Feeling that if I were to command respect, I had better first sharpen up my own reflexes, I spent the first few days firing at the clay pigeons that my men shot up for me. In this I was lucky that I was allowed a fairly generous allocation of cartridges. Because of the war they were almost unobtainable in the civilian world, and any farmer in the country would have given me a small fortune for the number I fired during that time.

However, the practice paid dividends for me. Used to guns, I had found little trouble in hitting two clay pigeons fired simultaneously. But I wanted to do better than this and soon found that by loading my twin barrelled shotgun and holding two extra cartridges in my mouth for quick re-loading, I was able to hit three and often four pigeons as fast as my operators could shoot them into the air.

It sounds like exhibitionism and no doubt some of it was, but there was more to it than that. I had heard that some of the cadets due shortly came from privileged families, and could be difficult and even arrogant when instructed by NCOs. I had met such young men in the past and found the one certain way to control them was to be so good at the thing one was teaching that they found it difficult if not impossible to match.

It certainly worked for me at Cranwell. When my cadets arrived and saw clay pigeons being blasted out of the air with such ease, the challenge to do as well fully occupied their minds. This served the purpose of the exercise and in turn provided me with well-behaved and respectful cadets.

So the first three weeks of August passed pleasantly enough, and although after nearly seven years in uniform I was itching to be a civilian again, with Shelagh waiting for me in the evenings and weekends, and with my work bringing me in contact with men of all creeds and classes, I was not finding Cranwell the odious place it had been in 1941.

But there was no way of shaking off the shadow of that Far-Eastern posting, for neither Shelagh nor I could forget that it had been cancelled only temporarily. Every day I arrived in the camp I half-expected an order to report to the Records Office and I must have rehearsed a hundred times in my mind what I would say to Shelagh if and when the news came.

The entire affair came to a head on the afternoon of the 26th. I'd had an easy day with only two classes of cadets and had slipped into the NAAFI for a cup of tea. As I was chatting to a colleague, the music on the radio stopped abruptly to make way for an important announcement. As we stopped talking and turned to listen, the announcement came in dramatic fashion. *'A bomb of massive explosive power has been dropped on the Japanese city of Hiroshima. The bomb, a new Allied weapon which releases the destructive power of the atom, has almost wiped the city out of existence and caused thousands of casualties. The Allied High Command is calling on the Japanese to surrender. If they do not, other cities will be destroyed in like manner. More news of this sensational development will follow later.'*

To me the stunning announcement was like the bomb explosion itself. In that moment I knew it not only signified the end of the war but the end of the world as we knew it. Nothing would ever be the same again. Like a switch being thrown on a railway track, it was one of those rare moments in history that diverts and changes mankind's entire destiny. I looked round to see the same emotion on the faces around me but it was not there. After an initial stir and a momentary buzz of interest, men were resuming the conversations they had broken off for the announcement.

I have never forgotten that reaction. Was it because men had become so blase, so used to death and destruction by this time, that not even this holocaust could disturb them? Or was it a failure of imagination to grasp the implications of this new weapon?

I could think of nothing else but the bomb for the rest of that day and my thoughts were in turmoil when I cycled home. What would the world do with it? What would it do to the world? The questions kept coming and coming, and yet one thought kept pushing in between them. If this bomb was so destructive that it could bring down the Japanese Empire, surely it would mean an end of postings to that theatre of war. Surely it must mean I would not have to abandon Shelagh for three more years.

A critic not alive during those days will instantly condemn me. Here was I, thinking of my self-interests when in Hiroshima thousands of my fellow men were dead or dying in agony. Put that way it does seem quite shameful. But what that critic must ask himself, with hand on heart, is the nature of his thoughts had he been one of the Allied servicemen massing to invade Japan. Military planners had already estimated that half a million of his kind would die before that country fell. What would he have done if he had been one of the many thousands of half-starved prisoners to whom the Japanese promised death the moment Allied troops landed on their beaches? Would he have foregone a weapon that might save his and their lives, particularly if he had been witness to the appalling atrocities the Japanese had carried out on his colleagues and friends?

He should also remember that if President Truman had not sanctioned the use of the bomb, not only would hundreds of thousands of Allied troops have been condemned to death but a countless number of Japanese too, and many of them women and children. The moralities of peacetime are a luxury that war does not allow. War is an obscenity and every military act is a choice between evils. All a man can do is choose the lesser of them, and his fellows can only hope it is the right one.

This is how we saw it and in the context of the time I cannot see we were wrong. Our sympathy for the stricken in Hiroshima was to come later when our survival was ensured. At the time we only thanked God that the interminable war seemed to be coming to an end at last. As history records, this merciful end came a few days later after the second atomic bomb was dropped on Nagasaki. A few days later, to my huge relief, my Far East posting was rescinded.

With the shadow of another long separation lifted, Shelagh and I were able to enjoy the remainder of that summer. We walked the country lanes searching for brambles, and when the crisp autumn mornings arrived, I picked mushrooms from the fields around my range and took them home to augment our rations which were as austere as at any time during the war.

Not that we cared about that. With the tension lifted, life was full of promise again. We laughed together when Shelagh, unused to gaslight, dusted the fragile mantle in our room and saw it disintegrate before her eyes. We laughed and sang at a Cranwell dance and recklessly wasted two whole shillings on the bus fare to Lincoln, where we visited the cathedral. We even treated ourselves again to the cinema: a wanton act made delicious by its very recklessness. In short the future seemed full of hope again and if life was austere what did it matter? The hedges had never been so red with berries and the trees had never looked more beautiful in their autumn colours.

But although austerity was bearable in the summer and autumn, it took on another aspect when the trees shed their leaves and the wind that I remembered from 1941 began to sob across the flat Lincolnshire fields. Because we were only tenants of the old ladies, our ration of coal was fixed at two bags a month. In vain I pointed out that my wife came from a warm climate and was feeling the cold more than the rest of us. Two bags were our ration and two bags was all we would get.

Not that Shelagh complained. Shelagh never complained about anything. But it was not long before I discovered she never lit the fire until I was due home and even then, if the ration were to last out the month, only two pieces of coal could be spared at a time. Her days were spent queuing in the cold for our rations, walking about the town to keep warm, or huddled up in blankets in our room.

I had to do something and a wooden fence near my skeet range offered one answer. Taking a hacksaw from one of my fitters — for some reason we couldn't obtain a larger saw — I began work on the fence, rendering the posts into lengths that would fit inside a kit bag. My men, all single and therefore living within the camp, wanted to help me but aware there would be severe punishment if complaints were made, I felt it unfair to involve them and so kept the fence my private felony.

The operation itself was relatively easy. The problem came when taking the kit bag home. Finding it too difficult to carry on the bicycle, I decided to plunder our piggy bank again so I could make at least two bus trips a week.

What proved surprising as Christmas approached and the fence became less than half its original size, was that no one seemed to notice and complain. At the same time, with wood burning so quickly and with winter getting a tight grip on the Lincolnshire countryside, the unhappy fence proved only a partial answer. Shelagh and I still had to sit huddled up in blankets at nights while we listened to the radio. I was only too aware that if Shelagh were to have even a tiny fire during the day, some other answer to heating had to be found.

Respite came when I was given four days leave for Christmas. After much thought we decided to be extravagant and spend the holiday with my parents. This meant taking a bus to Grantham and another connecting bus to Hull. To get a seat on a bus in those days was something a man dreamed about but seldom achieved. By the time the inevitable queue had wound its way inside, one was lucky to find standing room in the aisle, much less a seat.

But something very odd and disturbing happened this day. We actually found two seats vacant on the first bus we boarded. It should have been a moment of triumph, of dreams fulfilled, but there was uneasiness in the glance I gave Shelagh. Young though I was, I had already learned that life seldom offers such bounty without demanding a heavy price in return.

All was put right fifteen minutes later when the bus was heading down a country lane. There was a screech of metal, a bang, and we drew to a shuddering halt. The conductress conferred with the driver, then turned to her anxious wards. "Sorry but we've broken down. You'll all have to take the relief bus." As mutterings broke out and the packed aisle moved towards the door, her voice came again, this time with authority. "Mind you form a queue outside. I don't want any cheating. First out go to the front, the rest line up behind."

It was all clear to me now. Trapped in our rear seat, we had to wait until the bus unloaded itself, which meant by the time we debussed we were at the back of a long queue again. Thus when the relief bus arrived half an hour later and our turn came to clamber aboard we were back in our customary site standing in the aisle. As it started off and Shelagh was jolted against a fat lady, I gave her a reassuring smile. My fears had been groundless. Now I was restored to my destined place, we had every chance of a happy Christmas.

# THREE

The cold was bitter when we returned to Sleaford four days later, forcing me to step up my production of firewood. As the fence shrank and shrank, I began wondering what I would do when it vanished. There were no other fences in the vicinity: the fields were divided by hedges. During my off duty moments, I wandered through the huge camp to identify possible targets, but I could find nothing except wooden storage sheds and their like, and even in my circumstances I couldn't see myself sawing them down in full view of Cranwell's MPs.

So matters were coming to a crisis when one of my men pointed at one of the railway sleepers that we'd used as a base for the two skeet traps. "What about these? They'd burn well, wouldn't they?"

"Burn? They'd be perfect," I said.

He grinned at me. "So why don't you use 'em?"

"How can I? We're still using the traps."

"I don't mean these. I mean the ones we didn't use."

I gave a start of excitement. "You mean there are more?"

"There are nearly a dozen. Down in the shed near the armoury."

"Then fetch 'em," I said. "Get the others to help you and bring them up here."

This he did and the second part of Operation Firewood began. While I finished off the fence, my men borrowed a truck and brought ten sleepers up to the range. Feeling more secure once the remnants of the fence were no longer there to puzzle curious eyes, I began work on my first length of timber.

The trouble was I still had only the hacksaw and I can assure anyone who tries to cut up a railway sleeper into small logs with one, a man needs the muscles and patience of Hercules himself. By the time I had used up my sleepers my men had become as involved in my struggles as I was myself, and it was one of them who suggested a raid on the nearest coke store. With coke strictly rationed, this offered dangers beyond anything risked before, but with Shelagh back in Sleaford in a room like an ice box I was in no mood to draw back now. At the same time the problem must have affected my scruples because when two of my men offered to help, I accepted gladly.

So one dark night, armed with wire cutters and two shovels, we crept round the back of the coke bunker and snipped the fencing wire. Acutely aware that if Cranwell's MPs discovered us we were likely to be ceremoniously hanged, drawn, and quartered, we filled two kitbags with rustling coke. Then we repaired the protecting fence as best we could and man-handled the kit bags to the shed that had previously housed the sleepers. From there I would collect the kit-bags the following day.

With everything having gone like clockwork so far and deciding the devil looks after his own, I resolved to take one back home the following evening and the second the day later. In the meantime the second bag was hidden in the shed where the sleepers had been.

The following evening arrived and trying not to betray the weight of my burden, I heaved the kit-bag into the bus and jumped in after it. Seeing an empty seat, I heaved the kit-bag towards it and sank down with the bag between my knees. I had done well, I told myself.

It was only when the bus pulled away that my problems began. Decrepit and run down as most municipal transport was at that time, it thumped and bounced over every bump on the road and each time I could hear the coke rustling loudly inside the bag.

It did not seem to matter until I glanced round to see who was sitting behind me. At first I could see only civilians and half a dozen servicemen who were not taking the slightest notice of me. Relieved, I was about to settle back when I realized I had not glanced at the seat directly behind me.

I twisted my neck and froze. Two MPs, upright and self-righteous in their white caps and polished buttons, stared stonily back at me. In my haste to get the bag on board, I had not noticed them on entering the bus.

Afraid my shock had betrayed me, I swung back but at that moment the bus jolted again. This time the rustle of coke sounded like an Alpine avalanche. My imagination, no doubt sensitised by my near posting abroad, shot ahead of me and inflicted penalties way beyond the extent of my crime. Theft of military property!

Disgrace! Stripped of rank and thrown into the glasshouse! Perhaps separated from Shelagh for years and years! Why had I been such a fool?

The coke rustled again and this time I could feel two pairs of eyes boring into the back of my head. They knew, I told myself, and were playing a cat and mouse game with me! Why had I done it? Shelagh had warned me not to take such chances. Why hadn't I listened to her? Didn't I ever learn?

Never had a seven mile journey seemed longer. As we reached Sleaford, I braced myself. The bus kept stopping to drop off passengers but no one moved behind me. As we turned into London Road, I understood. They were waiting to make a sadistic arrest right in front of my home.

The bus stopped. I waited but no one moved. The mouse had to run before the cat leapt, I decided. Gritting my teeth, I rose, seized the neck of the kit bag, and dragged it towards the exit. No longer worrying about the rustling, I dropped the bag to the pavement and stood there, bracing myself as I waited for the axe to fall.

Instead I heard the double ting of a bell and saw the bus pulling away. Gazing after it in astonishment I saw the shaven necks of the MPs through the illuminated windows. Neither had even turned his head to follow my exit. It had all been in my mind. If I learned anything that day, it was that I most definitely was not the stuff of which criminals are made!

I was demobilized in March of that year. I received my last medical, my civilian suit, shoes, and hat, and a £60 gratuity for my six and a half years service. We paid our last rent to the old ladies, thanked them for having us, and took the bus back to Hull. As we stood in the bus aisle all the way, I felt reasonably certain that the storms and gales we had sailed through during recent years would now be giving way to calmer seas. It took me only a short time to discover how very wrong I was.

# FOUR

Having being given a short demobilization leave, I decided not to return to the Guildhall immediately but to spend the leave looking for an apartment. Although my parents were happy enough to give us a room again, their tiny house was not suited for two families and in any case our six months stay in Sleaford had given us a taste for our own home. So we spent the early spring days searching the city for a place we could call our own.

It proved an exhausting and frustrating task. Few cities in Britain had suffered the damage Hull had undergone during the war. Official reports said that 95 % of its buildings had received some degree of damage, and when one walked down its many streets as we did during the next fortnight, these statistics were easy to believe. Where buildings were not shattered ruins, they stood with sightless windows or leaking roofs, and refugees from the worst of these damaged homes had been re-housed in what spare accommodation had survived.

Indeed, the need for accommodation was so great that those in search of it had the right to requisition any empty property. Although this meant Shelagh and I possessed this right, it was precious little use in the circumstances.

In fact it all began to look hopeless until one evening we came across a large house on one of the main arterial roads. Although the windows of the adjacent properties were all boarded up, this house looked intact. Certain every room would be taken, we nevertheless climbed the steps to a large side door and rang the bell.

A tall, slim man in his late fifties, with thinning dark hair and a small moustache, answered our call. To our surprise, instead of the negative reply we expected, he told us to follow him through a large hall into a room at the front of the house. Here he introduced us to his wife, a small, bird-like woman who after saying 'good evening' and 'pleased to meet you' never spoke again throughout our interview. After shaking hands with her, we were invited to sit down and state our case.

We explained our position and our desire to have our own home.

In turn the man, whose name was Sharpe, asked me what my civilian work was. Showing interest when I told him, he then began asking Shelagh about her background. While she explained she was a South African who had recently come over to England to marry me, he went over to a gramophone and put on a record. As music filled the room, he turned to me and asked the name of the work.

In any other circumstances I would have told him where to go for his behaviour and walked out. I was already resenting his probing questions and this seemed a final insult. But the circumstances were not normal and we both knew this might be our last chance of a home. So, swallowing my pride, I told him it was Beethoven's Fifth.

This seemed to satisfy him and without glancing at his wife, he led us into the hall and up its winding staircase to two rooms at the rear of the house. One room was furnished as a sitting room, and the other, which had a communicating door, contained a double bed, a wardrobe and a dressing table. Although in both cases the furniture was Spartan, it was adequate, and the sitting room looked over a long if somewhat overgrown garden.

After showing us the rooms, Sharpe told us we could have the rooms for seventeen shillings a week and could move in the following Monday. He felt sure we would find the house quiet. Although he and his wife had two small children, they all lived downstairs.

We left unable to believe our luck. The house was conveniently situated, the two rooms were all we required, and although my Guildhall wage was going to be only two pounds, ten shillings a week, the rent was somewhat less than the going rate at that time.

Overjoyed, we returned to my parents and told them of our good fortune. Delighted for us, my mother offered to come and help Shelagh to spring clean the rooms after we moved in. For my part I decided that the vague dislike I had felt for Sharpe was unfounded: it was natural enough that he should want to vet would-be tenants before they shared the house with his family.

In short, after our long weeks of tramping the streets and envying every young couple who had a place of their own, we felt the clouds had rolled away and the sun was shining brightly again. We had not the slightest inkling at that time that we were two unsuspecting little flies about to enter the web of a very large and sadistic spider.

Helped by my father, we moved into the house on Monday morning. Sharpe met us at the door and was pleasant enough when I introduced my father. We carried our few possessions upstairs and spent the rest of the day walking about the rooms and enjoying the novelty of the situation. Although we'd had our own room at Sleaford, the fact I was still in the RAF had never allowed us a feeling of security. Now, after years of separation and another year of uncertainty, with our own rooms and I with a permanent job, it seemed that at last we could live like ordinary people everywhere.

Looking back today, it seems very naive to believe happiness comes in such simple terms. But we were young and we were also very tired of insecurity. We needed ground beneath our feet that would not slide away again. We wanted to know that tomorrow and the day after that we would awaken to find the familiar things still there. We wanted nothing else at that time but to have an undisturbed life in which we could enjoy the blessing of our reunion.

My first intimation that life was never going to be that placid came the very next day when I reported back for work. After being welcomed back by Pollard, the City Treasurer, I was told to report to my old office, the Wages and Superannuation Department, where its new chief, Gibson, would give me my duties.

Although the department had moved to a new and larger office at the front of the Guildhall, I was happy enough with the arrangement because two of my old colleagues, Johnnie Gemmell and Tommy Blackmore, who had been demobilized before me, were already working there. What I wasn't expecting was to be given exactly the same job I'd been doing seven years earlier: sticking stamps on insurance cards.

I made my protest to Gibson but he was not a man like my old boss, Frank Gosling, who had received promotion during the war and was now in charge of another department. Gibson was a man who never made a decision today if he could leave it until tomorrow. His method was to show sympathy and then to point out how much he'd like to help but . . . . His 'but' in my case related to the temporary staff who had been drafted in during the war and were now occupying the best jobs in the office. After all the loyal service they had given the Guildhall through those long war years of turmoil and disruption, how could he take away their jobs now? Was it fair? Couldn't I wait just a few weeks for him to sort something out?

It was the story millions of ex-servicemen must have heard at that time. The temporary staff had shown loyalty (the inference being that we, who had gone into the Armed Forces, had not), and it was neither fair nor convenient to displace them now. We would receive fair play eventually, but in the meantime we must be patient.

The devil of it was I could see a certain logic in it. Ex-servicemen, unless employed as non-combatants, had been trained in the martial arts, and these were hardly the skills employers were seeking. Moreover, that same training wasn't inclined to keep men passive if they felt exploited. In short, military training wasn't a quality employers were ecstatic about.

The outcome was I had little choice but to begin sticking on my insurance stamps again, thousands and thousands of them. I disliked it and I showed it at times, but I consoled myself with the thoughts of what might have been had our cards fallen in a different way. In other words I made the best of it, at least for the time being.

However, a second problem soon appeared. Since I'd returned to England I'd been having trouble with my neck. A sharp pain would suddenly develop in the nape and within half a hour my entire neck would lock. The pain would then become so severe that I would be unable to move my upper body and sometimes be unable to walk.

It had happened three times while I was at Cranwell. The first two times I had reported to the camp medical officer who had merely given me the usual aspirin mixture and excused me from duty for a couple of days. At the third occurrence, which happened only a few days before my demobilization, I had seen the local GP who had examined Shelagh the previous year. He had spent much more time on me and asked about my experiences in the Far East.

For some reason, perhaps because it was so long ago, I forgot to tell him about the damage I'd sustained from the German bomb in 1941. Instead his questions reminded me how I and others had suffered acute stiffness in the joints after being withdrawn from a particularly humid area in the Far East, to the extent we were hospitalized and given treatment. He said this present complaint was almost certainly a relapse of this condition and that once we were settled in Hull I should apply for physiotherapy.

During this appointment he spent a considerable time examining my back and chest and before I left he advised me to waste no time in seeing a doctor once I returned to Hull to have a complete physical check-up. At the time his advice had a concern and seriousness that puzzled me, but in the excitement of my discharge I soon forgot all about it.

There was no forgetting my neck, however. Perhaps because I was now sitting all day in unaccustomed postures, the attacks became more frequent. At first I tried to sit through them but the intensity of the pain soon made this impossible. I couldn't work, I could hardly bear to move my eyes, and on one occasion I had to be driven home, being unable to walk to the bus stop.

In the end Gibson, who, to give him credit, was extremely sympathetic, told me that the moment I felt the pain coming on I must tell him and then leave for home. As the initial pain gave me about thirty minutes warning before paralyzing me, I usually managed to get home in time.

I must have had at least two attacks during the next six weeks, which made me something of a liability in the office. They usually lasted about two days before I was fit to work again.

During this time Shelagh kept urging me to see a doctor and I kept procrastinating in the hope the attacks would cease. But eventually the need to provide medical evidence of them forced me into the waiting room of a local GP.

It proved to be one of the most shattering experiences of my life. In discussing my problem, I made some mention of the Sleaford's doctor's examination of my chest and back and his insistence I had a proper medical check-up. It was said more in humour than for any other reason, for apart from the neck problem I had been in excellent health for years. But it did lead to this doctor running his stethoscope over my chest. As he paused with it, I saw his expression change. "Do you say you've had good health? You've not suffered a shortage of breath or any other respiratory discomfort?"

I had that unpleasant premonition that such questions bring. "No. Nothing at all. Why?"

He moved his stethoscope over me again, listening intently. It must have been a full minute before he spoke again. "Didn't this doctor tell you why he wanted you to have a check-up?"

"No. I thought it had to do with my neck. Doesn't it?"

He ignored my question. "Didn't your RAF doctor say anything to you when you had your final medical?"

"No. Nothing."

He motioned me to sit down in a chair in front of his desk. He took a seat himself, sat looking at me for a moment, then seemed to come to a decision. "I'm sorry about this, laddie, but I've some bad news for you. Your heart is in quite a serious condition. I'm amazed you aren't conscious of it."

The world seemed to rock on its axis. "My heart? But it can't be. I've been in A1 category right throughout the war. I've flown much of the time. And my discharge book says I'm still A1."

"I'm sorry, laddie, but there's absolutely no doubt about it. Bad hearts are easy to spot. That's why I'm mystified your RAF doctor didn't mention it. You have a very sick heart."

I was now feeling cold from head to foot. "Can it be treated?"

He shook his head. "I'm afraid not."

I didn't like asking the question but circumstances demanded it. "How long have I got then?"

"That's something I can't say. It depends so much on what you do."

"But I must know. I've only been married a few months. I must know for my wife's sake."

He sighed. "Well, if you must know, I'd say about six months. Not much longer."

By this time I was certain I was having a particularly bad nightmare. "Six months! But surely there's something that can be done?"

"I only wish there was. If so I'd get treatment for you right away. But hearts can't be repaired. Someday, perhaps, but not yet."

"So there's no doubt about it and there is nothing that can be done?"

"I'm afraid that's the ticket, laddie. I'm desperately sorry. I only wish I could give you better news."

No words can express my feelings when I walked out into the street. I had escaped another posting to the Far East only to receive news that was far worse. A posting had at least offered a reasonable chance of returning to Shelagh. This news seemed to offer none at all.

# FIVE

I was panic stricken at the thought of telling Shelagh the news. I wanted to run away and find a hole to hide in. Then misery turned to anger. A bad heart surely couldn't happen overnight. I'd probably served with it for the last two or three years in the Far East when I could have had those years with Shelagh. Now I had only a few months left. Why hadn't they told me? I hated the entire world at that moment.

I could not tell Shelagh yet. Not after all she had sacrificed for me. I first made an appointment with another local doctor, only for him to tell me the same thing. I would only last six months if I took great care not to get excited or indulge in physical exercise. Convinced now, I knew I had to tell Shelagh that all she had given up for me was wasted. I did not just hate the world now. I think I hated the very faith my mother and my church had given me,

I can't remember Shelagh's reaction when I finally told her. It was too much of a blur in my memory. It was all so impossible to believe. Here was a strong, healthy-looking young man, with far more stamina than most of his kind, telling her his heart was so weak he had only a few months to live. It exploded all our hopes and dreams and left us in a nightmare world where happiness is an illusion and nothing could ever be trusted again.

If I had any doubts about the doctors' prognosis, they were quickly dispelled. With my neck still painful, I found it difficult to move but when I tried to get to my feet that evening, I felt my heart thudding in the most alarming fashion. Nor did the symptoms cease in bed that night. Unable to sleep, feverishly wondering what I should do and only succeeding in confusing myself further, I became aware of my heart pounding like an over-stressed piston. As I listened, I imagined irregularities that seemed to confirm everything I had been told.

Although memories are confused at this time, I believe we decided to say nothing to my parents. What we had to decide was what to do with our lives. As shock prevented either of us from thinking clearly, there seemed only one thing to do; to carry on as before until we could think clearly again.

None of this was helped by the problems we were having with Sharpe and the rooms we were renting from him but those I will relate later. At the time I had to decide what to do with my remaining months but what can one do when a salary has to be earned and bills to be paid? One can only continue as before and this is what I did. I returned to the Guildhall and if colleagues found me quieter than usual, I fobbed them off with one excuse or another. I don't remember feeling fear: perhaps I was too shocked. The days came and went and were meaningless. I went through the motions of living without feeling any of its emotions.

The question has to be asked why I did not try to see a specialist during this time. The answer lay in my symptoms. I could no longer run for a bus or my heart would race uncontrollably. I would walk up the winding staircase to reach our rooms at home and before I reached the landing an African drum would be pounding in my ears. I would bend down to pick something up and a lurch in my chest would make me believe my last moment had come.

In other words I had no reason to doubt my prognosis. I had received the opinions of two doctors and I was young and naive enough to believe in medical competence. There seemed no point in paying money, which we could not afford, to have yet another endorsement of my condition.

It was a short piece in the local newspaper that changed my mind. It said that a famous heart specialist was paying a visit to the city's general hospital. I don't remember the whys or wherefores but on a sudden impulse I decided to try to see him.

How I managed this I can't remember because I didn't make the appointment through my doctor. Perhaps I phoned the hospital and explained my situation. However it was done, he agreed to see me, and a week later I found myself in his surgery.

If memories of the previous weeks are fragmentary and blurred, memories of this day are crystal clear. He was a small wiry man in his fifties with crisp dark hair. He eyed me up and down as I entered his surgery, spoke a few reassuring words, and then told me to remove my shirt. Then, making measurements on my chest with some kind of pen, he began his examination.

Considering what rested on his decision, I felt little emotion. Perhaps by this time I was drained of it. He listened to my heart, he asked me questions, he made me do knee bends and touch my toes and listened to my heart again. Finally he put his stethoscope down in his desk and turned to me. He was smiling, something I could not understand.

"So you have been told you've a bad heart and not many months to live?"

I nodded. "Yes. Only a few months."

"How long was this ago?"

"About eight weeks. No, nine"

"And you believed it?"

"Yes."

"When did your symptoms start?"

I thought and then gave a start. "About the same time."

"Precisely." He walked forward and put a hand on my shoulders. "Now listen to me, my boy. There is absolutely nothing wrong with your heart. You could go outside and run a marathon and nothing would happen to you. Am I making myself clear?"

My face must have shown he was not. "You can't be serious."

"I've never been more serious. There is nothing whatever wrong with your heart."

"Then why did the doctors say what they did? There must be something wrong."

He shook his head. "No. The sound your doctors heard was caused by your lungs being more developed than most. Did you play a lot of sport before the war?"

I told him about the running and sprinting I had done and he nodded. "Then that probably accounts for it." He went on to use medical terms I have long forgotten, but the gist of it was that the sounds that had alerted my two doctors were innocuous and had nothing to do with my heart.

Hope was beginning to percolate into my mind, but at first only slowly. "Are you certain of this?"

He nodded. "That's going to be your problem, my boy. You've

had two doctors make an incorrect diagnosis and only one to tell you you're a very fit young man. Would you like to see another specialist to back up my findings?"

It was only then I understood what was happening. It was like a bomb bursting in my mind, flooding it with glorious Technicolor. "No," I said unsteadily. "I believe you."

"I hope you always will, my boy. Bad diagnoses of the heart can sometimes leave scars in a person's mind. If that happens, see another specialist right away."

At the time I hardly took notice of his warning, although I was to remember it in the years ahead. My reprieve was dazzling me and when he asked for the name and addresses of my two earlier doctors, the reason didn't register. I shook his hand, then went out into the street. Suddenly everything was different. On my arrival the day had been dull and rain had threatened. Now the sun was bright, the sky was blue, and every woman was beautiful. I heard myself laughing and saw people turn and stare at me, but what did I care? I didn't run along the pavements, I soared into the clouds and flew home with the birds. I was reborn. Shelagh had not wasted her life after all, and in my relief I told myself none of the matter-of-fact problems of life would ever bother me again. Such was my belief on that rare and magical day.

## SIX

Sadly, life has not given us the mental stamina to retain our gratitude for long. For a week Shelagh and I, intoxicated by our reprieve, laughed at every small problem we encountered. I stuck on my stamps with willingness, if not with joy, and smiled when my colleagues remarked at my change of mood. Shelagh sang as she did the housework and stopped worrying why we had not heard from her parents for some weeks.

But as our trauma fell behind us, the problems we had pushed aside began to re-assert themselves. Apart from my poor wages, the one that bothered us most was the atmosphere in our house. Shelagh had mentioned it first to me, no doubt because she spent more time in it than I, but soon I began to feel it too.

It was a thing difficult to describe. Although Sharpe was right and the house was quiet, it was not a peaceful silence. Instead it had a strange baleful quality that suggested something or someone was waiting to harm us.

At first we both laughed at ourselves. Neither of us, and particularly Shelagh, were prone to such imaginings and we might have shaken them off if Shelagh hadn't noticed she was being watched every time she descended the stairs to go out. Not openly but from the shadows of a doorway or behind the staircase. In the main she believed it was the bird-like woman spying on her although occasionally she thought it was Sharpe himself. By this time we had learned he was a retired policeman and so he was home most days of the week.

I didn't know what to think. Apart from knowing Shelagh was the last person in the world to imagine such things, I had caught glimpses of eyes watching me when I moved about the house. Yet there seemed no reason why we should be watched. We paid our rent regularly and to our belief had not caused the slightest trouble. We had not even had more than three or four visits from friends because, in our earlier belief our time together was limited, we had wanted to be alone together as much as possible.

A further mystery was our lack of mail. When we had been

living with my parents, Shelagh had received a letter from her mother almost weekly. Yet since our move she had received only two letters, and one of those was from her sister in America. From these letters we discovered Mrs McGrath was shortly to sail for England and Monica was planning to arrive soon afterwards. Mrs McGrath would stay with us for a week or two until Monica arrived and then the two of them would move down to London to meet my brother.

Although neither were to blame, and although I was delighted that Shelagh was going to be reunited with her mother again, the truth was that neither Mrs McGrath nor Monica had the slightest idea what Britain had suffered during the war, and although I knew my parents and my brother would do their best, neither of us could see how they could cater for them in their limited accommodation. So Shelagh and I decided we had only one option: to ask Sharpe if he would allow us to rent the empty front bedroom that stood on our landing. It was fully furnished with a double bed and would be ideal for the two women while they stayed with us.

After the mysterious spying we had been subjected to, we were surprised how accommodating Sharpe was when we made our request. He told us we could have the bedroom for a further seven shillings a week provided we took it from the present date.

Although it meant a cut in our living standards for longer than we planned, we were only too willing to agree. In fact I remember feeling guilt for our earlier suspicions of the man and his family.

Apart from the mysterious dearth of mail, nothing of any significance happened until the night before Mrs McGrath arrived. Around seven o'clock Sharpe knocked on our sitting room door, drew me aside, and told us he needed the bed from the front room for a friend. When I pointed that we had been renting the room for weeks and my mother-in-law was arriving the following day, he shrugged and said it couldn't be helped. His friend needed it urgently and would be coming for it that night. With that he walked away.

At first Shelagh couldn't believe it when I told her. "How can he do that the very night before she arrives? Why didn't he give us more warning?"

All my suspicions were back. "It's deliberate. He's waited until the last minute to make things as awkward as possible for us."

It was always difficult for Shelagh to think ill of anyone. "But why should he do that? We've never done him any harm. What possible reason could he have?"

I was disturbed as well as angry. I had the feeling this was only the beginning. "Perhaps he gets a kick out of this kind of thing. Perhaps he's a pervert."

She wasn't convinced but either way we had to move fast. Although it was quite late, we took a bus round to my parents and explained our dilemma. As I expected, they immediately offered to lend us the bed from their spare bedroom. My father solved the problem of moving it by getting permission to use his van the following morning. At this time he was working for a sweet wholesaler and delivering items of confectionery to shops in a 15 cwt van. For myself I took a couple of hours off work and the two of us carried the bed upstairs. Sharpe came out of his sitting room as we were crossing the hall and his momentary look of disappointment told me my suspicions were correct. It was difficult to believe a man could do such a petty and ridiculous thing to a couple who had never harmed him, but after that look I was certain I was right.

Concerned what he might do next, I was tempted to have it out with him there and then but knew that for Shelagh's sake I must avoid any further trouble until her mother had been and gone. So I swallowed back my resentment and installed the bed ready for her arrival.

She arrived by taxi around 7 pm the next day. Because I had been unable to take the time off work, she had arranged for a friend to meet her off the ship in Southampton and escort her up to Hull.

After a joyful re-union, Shelagh showed her mother her room and I asked her companion, a man at least twenty years her junior, if he minded sleeping on the sofa in our sitting room. When he, an ex-sailor who had met Shelagh's parents during the war, laughed at my apologies, we spent the next few hours catching up with our news.

We retired around midnight and all went well until the following morning. As it was Saturday we had decided to take Mrs McGrath round to my parents, whom she had never met, and we set out soon after breakfast. As we were descending the staircase I saw Sharpe was standing on a chair in the hall, ostensibly changing a bulb in the chandelier. Thinking I had better keep some kind of social contact going, I took Mrs McGrath over to introduce her.

What happened next sounds unbelievable in its context. Lowering the light bulb, he stared down at Mrs McGrath and her friend and then said in the most offensive way possible: "And where did the two of you sleep last night?"

It was such a preposterous remark that for a moment I felt I must be wrong and he was only inquiring if the two had been comfortable. But when I heard Shelagh give a gasp and then a cry of protest, I knew he had meant it as an insult.

Somehow I controlled myself long enough to ask the three of them to leave the house. When they reluctantly left, with Mrs McGrath looking shocked and upset, I turned to Sharpe and demanded an explanation.

I was too angry to remember his exact words but in effect they were full of puritanical criticisms about our right to use his house for immoral purposes.

It was more than enough for all my suspicions to blaze into life. Until now he had been weighing us up and biding his time. Now, with Mrs McGrath's arrival, he was in a position to inflict the maximum embarrassment on us and this was his first open move. I will not repeat what I said to him that morning but they left him in no doubt of my feelings,

The result of his insult meant that Mrs McGrath, believing her arrival had caused the quarrel, wanted to leave immediately and move down to London. But naturally enough Shelagh wanted more time with her and was also worried how she would manage in London on her own with my brother away in a repertory show. So we insisted she stayed with us at least until Monica arrived or until my brother returned home. She finally agreed but she was so upset by Sharpe that when she was not with us or when we had to go out, she kept herself locked in her room. It was a sad and distressing time for her when it ought to have been a happy one.

Now that my suspicions were white hot, I began making serious enquiries about our mail. Until now, although it had seemed unlikely, we had excused its lack or paucity on our friends' and relations' neglect. Now we discovered they had all answered our letters and in turn been puzzled by our complaints.

To test our suspicions, we asked a local friend to write us on a certain day and waited to receive the letter the following morning. Our original arrangement with Sharpe had been for him to place our mail on a small table near the front door. No letter was present that morning but it appeared on the second day, which made me check the envelope. Although the job had been expertly done, we were certain the flap had been steamed open and closed again. It seemed that even the letters allowed to reach us were read beforehand.

Proof of this came to us in a most dramatic way a couple of weeks later because of an enterprise we were involved in. Since I had returned to the Guildhall, the boredom of my job had driven me to think of some other way of making a living and I had hit on the idea of opening a Record Library shop. Gramophone records, as they were known in those days, were in desperately short supply because of the war, and it had occurred to me that if one could obtain enough second-hand ones and loan them out as books are loaned out, there might be a robust demand for them.

I had discussed the idea with Shelagh and she thought it a good one. But there were problems. The first was money. We had only sixty-six pounds in our account and that would hardly be enough to buy an adequate number of records, much less to provide the facilities to display them. For that we would need a shop, and as most of the unoccupied shops were bomb-damaged and windowless, this would clearly be a huge problem in itself, without taking into account the cost of fixtures and fittings.

However, with my need to occupy myself with something more than sticking on insurance stamps, I approached Des Matthews. To my delight both he and Vee liked the idea, and offered to put an equal amount of money into the venture. Feeling this might just be enough if we improvised with fixtures and fittings, the four of us began searching for a suitable shop and for well-preserved records.

To our surprise we found the latter relatively easy to obtain, possibly because hardship had driven some wives to sell their record players while their husbands were in the Forces. Our small advertisement in the local newspaper brought in dozens of replies and soon we were spending our evenings taking the bus hither and thither to addresses all over town where we were often offered piles of records for a few pounds a time.

However, while obtaining records was relatively easy, transporting them home and stock piling them was another matter. As Des and Vee had no space for them, we decided to store them in a cupboard in Mrs McGrath's bedroom. This we were able to do because not only did she agree to it but she also kept her door locked because of Sharpe's behaviour. Conscious that letting out records on loan was a new venture, I felt certain Sharpe would try to spoil it in some way if he guessed our intention. Consequently Des and I were very careful not to let him see our purchases when we bought them round in the evenings.

Finding a suitable shop proved a huge problem. We roamed the bomb-damaged streets, we tried estate agents, and I made enquiries from the Guildhall's Housing Department, but all in vain. In the meantime our stocks of records grew larger and larger. By this time Monica was due in England and, because of Sharpe, Mrs McGrath had sent her a message to go straight to my brother's flat in London and not to come to Hull. It meant Shelagh would not meet her sister but there seemed no alternative.

So, no doubt with secret relief at her escape from that unhappy house, Mrs McGrath bade us farewell and left for London. It was a sad and distressing moment for Shelagh and as I watched her kiss her mother goodbye I remember wondering how many more heartbreaks this wonderful girl would have because of her relationship with me. I was not long in finding out.

## SEVEN

Although the rent for the spare bedroom was a drain on our limited income, we had to keep paying it because otherwise, under the current housing laws, Sharpe could have ejected us. As it happened however, we still needed it for the storage of the records. The problem remained the shop in which to display them and offer them on loan. At last, and somewhat ironically, we finally obtained one not a quarter of a mile from Sharpe's house. We were shown inside it by the agent. It consisted of two rooms, one large frontal one and a smaller one behind. Both rooms were ankle deep in soot and pieces of masonry, and its one-time front window no longer existed, being boarded up by wooden planks.

But it was a shop and it stood on the main road near enough from our accumulated stock of records to make their removal a relatively easy matter. The rent, which was twenty-five shillings a week, was something we could just about afford, and so we took it and decided to worry later about how we could refurbish it.

Our first task was to get rid of the soot and the rubble, a job that took us two weeks. Then we had to find some way of displaying our records. We knew we would need shelves but the records could not just be piled upon them: they would need keeping separate for identification purposes. So finally I hit upon the idea of using white cord as separators with the records standing upright between them. This seemed the cheapest method possible.

But first we needed the shelves. By this time we had collected two thousand classical and light classical records and over two thousand 'pop' records, and by allowing an inch between each, we estimated we would need four tiers of shelves around each of the two rooms.

We bought the necessary wood but neither Des nor I were carpenters and we knew it was more than likely that if we did the job ourselves, it would look amateurish if not downright shoddy. So not for the first or the last time in my life, I asked my father for his help.

He came in his usual willing way and for the next two weeks

spent his evenings sawing the shelves to the right sizes and attaching them to the walls. We helped him all we could and in between times we catalogued the records, which was no small task in itself. Our plan was to have the opera, the classical and light classical works in the front room and the pop recordings in the rear one. We kept to this plan when the shop was eventually ready.

But firstly there were the holes to drill through the shelves and the cord to be threaded through them. The holes had to be drilled by hand, and thousands were needed. Afterwards the shelves were erected and the threading of cord began.

It was a hilarious as well as a messy task. In all we estimated we used three miles of cord. We spent seven evenings just threading that cord in and out and before the job was completed I think we all had nightmares of being trapped and tied up in a huge spider's web. But it was done at last and with hundreds of lines of parallel white cord running through the varnished shelves, the effect was both neat and attractive. I remember an old lady peering through the doorway one day and seeing the shelves and string before the records were introduced. She examined them and then turned to Shelagh, her eyes wide behind her spectacles. "Oh, my dear! What an enormous amount of work you must have put in." How very right she was.

All we had to do now was furnish the two rooms and then bring in the records. With our money all spent, we carpeted the floors with underfelt and set up a hand-wound record player in the centre of the front room, both borrowed from Des's parents. With my parents lending us a couple of small tables and a chair for the shop manager to use, we were ready to bring in the records. Shelagh, bless her, volunteered to be the shop manager.

But before we began transporting the records, Shelagh received an extraordinary letter from her father in Cape Town. It came only a few weeks after Mrs McGrath's departure to London. After losing so many letters, its very presence on the downstairs table was an occurrence in itself, but we had only to read it to understand why Sharpe had placed it there.

It was a letter full of concern and distress from Shelagh's father asking what on earth was happening to 'mother' while she was staying with us. Why was she being locked up in her room all day long? Why were Shelagh and I behaving so badly towards her? Why were we having wild parties and orgies in the house? Why had our landlord felt obliged to write and warn him about our behaviour? What in heaven's name had happened to the two of us?

*'Pop' (Mr. McGrath: Shelagh's Father)*

It took some time for Shelagh and I to believe anyone, even Sharpe, could go to such lengths, and it was only another airmail from her father explaining it had been a letter from Sharpe himself that had contained these complaints that convinced us he was the culprit. While Shelagh hastily scribbled an airmail letter back to her father telling him it was all nonsense, I made enquiries from my friends and learned they too had received similar stories about our behaviour, although in their cases the scurrilous letters had been typed and unsigned.

All this explained where our missing letters had gone. At another time and place it would have all seemed stupid and pointless, if not downright comical. As I told our friends I only wished I could have afforded an orgy, but with every spare penny going into the record project, I had barely enough over to afford a glass of beer.

It all led to my challenging Sharpe but, as I expected, he denied all knowledge of the letters, saying instead that people get the enemies they deserve and with my personality I must have plenty of those.

Although the letters to my friends caused nothing but amusement, the one to Shelagh's father was a different matter altogether. Yet when I approached a lawyer for advice he told me that even if my wife's father sent us a copy of the scurrilous letter it would not be sufficient to penalize Sharpe. Only Mr McGrath's personal presence in court could do that, and at that time it was not possible for him to make the journey.

In other words, Sharpe's knowledge of the law had enabled him to assess how far he could take his persecution without any risks to himself. Indeed, as Shelagh warned me one evening, I was the one in danger now because, not being fully rehabilitated from the war and possessing a psychological hatred of bullies, I could well get into trouble myself if I ever lost my control and struck him. It was a warning that made me wonder if this was his plan.

If so he nearly had his wish only a few days later. I cannot remember what his new provocation was that made me go looking for him, but when I found him he was out in his garden digging up potatoes. In the quarrel that followed he made some sneering remark that all we ex-servicemen were the same and I was just like the other cowards who had fled from France in 1940.

I can't fully explain the effect this sneer had on me because I had in no way been involved in the Dunkirk evacuation. Perhaps it was just that by this time the Mr Hyde in me had taken too much from this psychopath. Suddenly I saw myself grab the spade from him and in the next moment bring it down with fearful force on his head. Before my eyes his head split open like a melon as the spade sliced down and buried itself into his neck.

I stood motionless as the gruesome remains tottered and then collapsed on the upturned soil. I wish I could say I felt regret but at that moment Mr Hyde was quite ready to bury the creature's remains in unconsecrated soil and walk away whistling. After all, he argued, millions of good men and women had been killed during the last few years and I might have killed a few of them myself. This pervert helped a little to restore the balance.

It was then I felt my arm being tugged and heard Shelagh's frantic voice. As Mr Hyde disappeared back into his cave and my eyes cleared I saw Sharpe was still standing before me. Only now his sneer had gone. He had seen death in my face and knew he was lucky to be alive. Without a word he turned and half-ran back to the house.

I was trembling like a shell-shocked man, unable to decide which vision was the true one. It took Shelagh to reassure me. "It's all right, darling. You didn't strike him." Then her voice broke. "But we must get away from this awful place. As soon as we can."

I knew how right she was. I knew I would never be able to control Hyde a second time. Sharpe knew it too because for days I never saw him and our mail began to appear on the hall table again. But I knew he was only biding his time. Unable by law to give us notice, he was waiting for an occasion when he could strike us without danger to himself. It was some weeks before that chance came.

In the meanwhile Shelagh had told my parents about my garden affair. Recognizing its urgency, they approached the Housing Department to see if they could exchange their tiny house for one that could accommodate us all. Such exchanges were possible at that time and the Department put our names down on their urgent waiting list.

It was no small sacrifice for my parents to make because my father, a gardener by nature, had tended his present plot with loving care. But gestures of this kind were so much a part of their natures that one almost took them for granted. Even so, the move took time and while waiting we spent our spare time preparing our Record Library for our opening day

It was during this time that I learned from Sharpe's neighbours that since his retirement he had become a private detective who specialized in obtaining evidence of extra marital activities for divorce procedures. The discovery did not surprise me in the least. He seemed ideally suited for such distasteful work.

At the same time I could not forget my experience with him in the garden. My hatred had been so intense that in my mind I had killed him with pleasure. Surely I had over-reacted. If so, why? Was it because of what he was doing to Shelagh? After all her sacrifices I had desperately wanted to give her some happiness in England and yet everything so far seemed to have conspired against us. Having to share our first real home with a pervert seemed so cruel that I wanted to strike out at the world.

Yet was it only that, I asked myself? Had the war changed me? Had it taken from me the trust I had once had in my fellow men? Was I becoming a bitter and disillusioned man not fitted to share his life with such a girl as Shelagh?

It would be a lie to say these thoughts obsessed me. They came and went according to the mood of the day. But that terrifying moment when I believed I had killed Sharpe haunted me and I kept telling myself that I must never lose control like that again.

# EIGHT

Monica, whom I had not met before, came up north to see us less than a week after my fracas with Sharpe. It was no problem recognizing that she and Shelagh were sisters. Although she was a couple of inches taller than Shelagh and had darker hair, she too had inherited the beauty and graceful carriage of her mother, and it was easy to see why both girls had been offered film trials before the war when their mother had brought them to England on holiday. Shelagh had laughingly declined hers but Monica, having had stage ambitions like my brother, had stayed on to study at RADA. From England she had gone over to the States, only for the European war to break out shortly afterwards. When America had entered it in 1941 she had joined the Army Entertainment Corps and had served in it until August 1945. Her plans were now to spend a short holiday with her mother in England and then to return with her to South Africa.

Although she had only intended a brief visit, she was happy to see Shelagh again and knowing Raymond would take care of her mother, she decided to stay with us for a few days to meet my parents and to see our shop which was almost ready for its opening. She also saw the damage Hull had sustained during the war and her shock and distress made me realize that, in spite of the newsreels, how little Americans knew of the damage Britain had suffered.

Although Sharpe had been quiet since our episode in the garden, both Shelagh and I feared he might begin some new gambit now Monica had arrived. She had, of course, already been told about him by her mother but at first found it difficult to believe anyone could act so maliciously until she was shown her father's letter. "But why? Why on earth did he tell such lies," she asked. "Had you had some serious quarrel with him? Do you owe him money or had you broken something he values?"

Shelagh shook her head. "We hadn't done a thing to him. We never have. He just started off by insulting mother and he hasn't let up since."

"But then it doesn't make any sense. Is he mad?"

"We've wondered ourselves. But it doesn't seem that way when you talk to him. Neither of us can understand what his motive is."

After reading the letter Monica wanted to see him but Shelagh was against it. I knew her reason. She didn't want me dragged into another confrontation. "Leave it, Monica. Fred's mother and father are hoping to get a larger house and then we will be free of him."

We said goodbye to Monica two days later. Her destination was my brother's flat in London. He had recently moved to a larger one in Camberwell and so now had the room to accommodate both her and her mother.

I knew that for Shelagh it was an emotional goodbye because with Monica and her mother sailing to South Africa after a couple of weeks, she had no idea when she would see them again. It was true that with South Africa calling for immigrants, we had put our names on a waiting list earlier that year, but it had been more of a gesture than an intention, a covering of our bets, so to speak. At the time we had no thought of leaving the country.

So we said our goodbyes to Monica with some regret, although I believe we both felt relief that her visit had not been marred in some way by Sharpe's malice.

Less than three weeks later my parents received permission to move into a larger house. For us it was like a reprieve from prison, although we now had to find the money for the removal of our bits and pieces of furniture. Here we were helped by my grandmother of all people. An old lady now, living with her younger daughter Lena and her husband in Bridlington, she had suddenly decided to give her three grandchildren, Raymond, myself and Freda a hundred pounds each. It was an entirely unexpected gesture but with our finances at zero after the expense of the shop, it was a minor godsend.

It had one proviso, however. My hundred was to be reduced to eighty-five pounds because she was using fifteen pounds of it to pay off the remains of my parents' bankruptcy debts. Why she docked the full amount from my gift I never knew, but for my part I was only too pleased that the debts for which my mother had suffered through no fault of her own were closed at last. We still had enough money from the gift to pay for our furniture removal and to help

Des and Vee to put the last touches to our shop.

The day we finally left that unhappy house can never be forgotten. Johnnie Gemmell, my friend from the Guildhall, was with us. As the last of our pieces of furniture were carried into the removal van, I saw Sharpe's wife peering at us from one of the side windows. There was no sign of Sharpe himself. I had half expected him to cause some obstruction to our movements, but we saw nothing of him that morning. When we finally closed the side door and walked to the waiting van I think we both felt like escapees from prison. We had no way of knowing that our persecutor had not finished with us yet.

The house my parents had been given was in a residential part of the city and large enough for two families. Freed of Sharpe's influence, Shelagh could be heard singing again and even I found the sticking of stamps on insurance cards less of a chore. Appropriately my old office boss, Frank Gosling, added his contribution to our new life. With the survivors of his staff now back from their wartime duties, he invited us all to spend an evening with him at the historical Hull Fair.

Forbidden during the war years, the Fair was now making its comeback and Corporation Field was once again crowded by puffing steam engines, big Dippers, roundabouts, Romany fortune tellers, and the exotic rest. With the fair having sentimental memories for most of us, Frank Gosling added to them that night. Blackmore, Blackburn, Johnnie Gemmell, and Claude Brown were all there with their wives or fiancés: the only ones missing were 'Nobby' Clarke who had been killed during the 1944 invasion and Frank Gosling's wife who had died during the war.

I found it a very special occasion. To date I had only encountered Frank Gosling as a stern but highly efficient departmental boss. I had respected him for it but in the way of the young, I had found fault with his strict discipline. It was true he had written me during the war to wish me luck, but still in my mind he was the unapproachable disciplinarian.

But this night he was one of us: laughing, joking, buying us drinks, a warm and lovable human being. It was a happy occasion and made better because of its contrast to the general austerity of the time. We rode on the Shamrocks, slid down the Great Tower, teetered on the Cake Walk, and tried our luck on the gambling stalls. Then, as the evening wore on and the myriads of lights shone and sparkled through the autumn dusk, we retired to a bar in Walton Street and began swapping yarns in the way of reunions.

As the stories were told, Gosling, who was clearly impressed by Shelagh's beauty, kept on buying us rounds of rum. I lost count of the number after the sixth but we all seemed able to walk relatively upright when the evening finally ended. No doubt like everything else at that time, the rum was well below strength.

But, without indulging in self-pity, it did seem Shelagh and I could not have any enjoyment during those days without having to pay for it. On our way home she discovered her gold watch was missing. As it was the only thing of any value we possessed, it was a disappointing ending to an evening that until then had shown such promise.

We had one more memorable evening that week before Sharpe returned to our lives. With most of its surviving ex-pupils now demobilized, my old grammar school held a re-union party. Shelagh and I went, along with Stewart Cottingham who had come to spend a few days with us in our new home.

I found it a bitter-sweet occasion. Until then I had not known the casualty list of ex-pupils but now learned it was much higher than I had expected. In all, forty-six had been killed. To make things worse, because we had been the ideal age for military service in 1939, many of them came from my own grade and I discovered I would never see friends like Haydn West, Jack Buchanan, Ray Rountree, and John Batterbee again.

One incident will always remain in my memory. Shelagh and I had no sooner entered the large gymnasium where the re-union was being held when I heard a cry and the next moment a beautiful eighteen year old girl ran towards me, threw her arms around my neck, and after kissing me, sobbed as if her heart would break

At first I did nor recognize her but as her sobs died down I learned she was Haydn West's younger sister. She had only been a child of eleven in the days when Haydn and I had been friends but it seemed she had always liked me, and after her brother's death had made enquiries about me, only to be told that I had been killed too. I found her relief at discovering that not all her childhood friends had died very moving. Nothing seemed to display more the misery and obscenity of war.

So passed the first week of our escape from Sharpe. It was, however, not long before his baleful influence returned once more.

## NINE

Now settled in our new home, Shelagh and I were able to devote our spare time to the shop. With my Guildhall work so lacking in both interest and prospects, I think we both saw the shop as our hope of a better future.

But although we were alive with new optimism it was only a few days before a brown envelope came through the letter box. We read its contents with disbelief. It was a letter from a lawyer telling us that Sharpe had filed a complaint that we had deliberately defaced the walls of our rooms before moving house and that unless we recompensed him by paying thirty-five pounds we would be taken to court.

It was a totally unexpected ploy and caught us by surprise. Having decorated the rooms ourselves, they were in excellent condition when we left, as Johnnie Gemmell could testify. At the same time it put us in a cleft stick. Thirty-five pounds was beyond our means even if to avoid a court case we decided to submit to the claim. Yet on the other hand, if we allowed the case to go to court we might still have to pay a lawyer's fees. Either way it would be money we could not afford. which was undoubtedly the reason Sharpe was telling the lie.

My feelings could be imagined. To pay the money, even if we could have afforded it, was unthinkable and yet I had Shelagh to consider. She had never been in a court case in her life and although she laughed at my fears I could not forget that since her arrival in England nothing had gone right for her. Instead of bringing her happiness our marriage seemed to have done the very reverse. As I could not believe that even Sharpe could want to harm a girl like her, I felt certain I was the object of his malice. But without giving way to him and trying to borrow the money, I could only take her advice, which was wait and see what happened, and in the meantime concentrate on the shop.

It was ready in early December. The records stood between their white cord separators with card labels below giving each its name and performer. A thick book with cross-references allowed any record to be found quickly no matter how a customer's request was phrased. Our borrowed gramophone stood in the centre of the front room and a table and chair stood behind it to accommodate Shelagh. As this meant she could not seek employment as Vee had done, it was agreed she would receive a small wage as our compensation.

Only two things were needed now. One was a name for the shop and the other a decision on borrowing charges. As it was a new venture we thought THE RECORD LIBRARY explained its purpose and had a poster printed and affixed to the frontal boards. Record charges were less easy to estimate because we had no idea how careful or careless our customers would be. In the end we settled for 6d a record for three days. This was for individual records. For opera sets, of which we had five, we would charge five shillings for the same period.

*The Record Library premises*

We were now ready to open but how could we alert the public about the venture? Having scraped the barrel to get this far, there was no way we could afford to advertise on the scale required. We discussed the problem at length and Des wondered if we could not use the shop's novelty as a publicity item. Accordingly we phoned the local newspaper and asked to speak to its chief reporter.

As we had hoped he was quite excited by the idea and the very next day sent a reporter/photographer round to take pictures of the shop both inside and out. We made sure Shelagh was in attendance and, as I expected, her composure and good looks earned her as many photographs as the shop itself! Clearly impressed by it all, the reporter left us with the assurance that the project would receive a centre page coverage in the following Friday newspaper, which was the major edition of the week.

Shelagh and I received our court order a few days later. Not receiving his financial demand, Sharpe had in some way brought his case forward. As we were both to attend the magistrate's court the following Tuesday, we had no option but to postpone the shop opening until the case was over.

Although we could ill afford it, I now had to seek the advice of a lawyer. He told me to send a friend to view the allegedly defaced rooms and I asked Johnnie Gemmell to do us the favour. He returned to tell us that the wallpaper of both our living rooms and Mrs McGrath's old room was torn and heavily disfigured with soot.

This was the substance of the case the following Tuesday. Sharpe brought with him a witness who claimed he had seen our rooms before and after our removal and there was no doubt we had deliberately defaced them. In turn Johnnie Gemmell told the court he had helped us move from the rooms and could swear on oath we had left them intact.

Thus the case more or less rested on which witness was believed, and as a consequence the cross-questioning lasted the entire morning. It only ended when Sharpe's wife entered the witness box and said the walls looked as if a broom dipped in soot had been run up and down them. At this point the magistrate glanced at Shelagh and said he could not see such a well-bred young lady doing anything so spiteful. Indeed, he went on dryly, it did seem that Mrs Sharpe was better acquainted with the method of defacement than any of the accused. After a few more acid comments aimed at the Sharpes, he dismissed the case.

Greatly relieved, we left the courtroom. As we stood chatting to Johnnie in the main hall, Sharpe approached us, his face pale and vindictive. He addressed himself to Johnnie. "Do me a favour, Mr

Gemmell. Please give your wife my warmest regards. While you were away during the war, I used to see a great deal of her when I was on duty in East Hull. She always had an open door for us policemen."

It was said in a way that could have only one connotation. In other circumstances I might have struck him and landed myself in another court case. But for once his detective work was flawed. Although the female in Johnnie's home was listed as Mrs Gemmell, she was his mother, not his wife. Johnnie was a bachelor.

Until that moment I don't think even Johnnie, an old friend, had believed everything we had told him about the man's extraordinary behaviour. Now it was seen in the flesh, so to speak. When Johnnie dismissed him with a few well chosen words, I could only hope he would not suffer himself in the future. Fortunately this did not happen.

For our part, although we had won the case, we still had lawyer's fees to pay and so in that sense Sharpe's action had still hurt us. It made me realize that if a persecutor had the money and was careful enough to disguise his reason, he could harm or even ruin an impoverished man by simply trumping up false charges. It left me wondering if this was to be his new ploy or whether he would seek some other way of taking his revenge for his lost legal action. It so happened we were not long in finding out.

In the meantime our attention returned to the shop. While Shelagh prepared to open it, we all awaited the newspaper article that we felt held such promise. When Friday evening arrived I hurried out of the Guildhall to find the nearest paper boy. Grabbing the evening edition from him I opened it eagerly, to find the centre page. I reached it and then froze.

There was nothing, absolutely nothing about our shop or about the venture itself. Puzzled and disappointed, I scanned the entire paper but there was no mention anywhere. Finding a phone box I contacted Des, to discover he was as puzzled as I.

Feeling it could only be some error I tried to phone the reporter at his office. He had gone home but I was given his number. I phoned him there later after I had told Shelagh about the article's omission and his answer was rueful. Yes, he had written up the article and passed it with appropriate photographs to the chief editor. That was the last he had heard of it.

Naive on such matters, I asked why. He had agreed it was the first record library in the country and so was extremely newsworthy. Then why had the editor not printed it?

His voice told me he was embarrassed. Was I not aware that the owner of the largest music shop in the city was a member of the same club and lodge as his editor? Of course, the coincidence might have no bearing whatever on the article's omission but in the circumstances it might be wise to pay in the future for the news of our venture rather than rely on the goodwill of the editor.

In other words he was telling me the omission was due to the old boy's network. A wealthy businessman had discovered a couple of young ex-servicemen had thought of a venture that might infringe his monopoly and his profits. The war hadn't been fought for that kind of nonsense. Not on your life it had not. So lift the phone and have a private word with your newspaper colleague

I believe that at first the four of us took the omission philosophically. Perhaps free publicity had been too much to expect. After all, we were in the business world now where one could expect no favours. We would have to grit our teeth and do it the hard way. At least no one could stop us doing that, or so we thought.

So we penned out an advertisement, pooled our pennies, and asked Vee to insert the advert in the Monday newspaper, the same day that Shelagh was to open the shop.

Looking back on it we could hardly have chosen a worse time to open a new venture. It was the winter of 1947, that infamous winter when ice was five inches deep on lakes and ponds and the icicles from the eaves of our new lodgings reached down to the yard a full twenty-five feet below. Pavements bore rutted snow as hard as cement. In the Guildhall we were working in thick pullovers and in candlelight, as were men and women in other city offices. The country's coal stocks had been exhausted by the demands of the invasion and yet the Americans had now switched their aid to Germany instead of to their wartime ally. Men and women were beginning to wonder if it were not better to lose wars than to win them.

Yet in spite of the conditions and the totally inadequate coal ration given to the shop, Shelagh insisted on opening it to set the ball rolling. Once the advertisement appeared in the paper she felt sure the customers would be attracted and our hard work would be rewarded. So in conditions totally alien to her, she took the key on the Monday morning and, while I made for my Guildhall office, she made for the shop.

I had barely settled down at my desk before she phoned me. She had reached the shop but could not insert the key into the Yale lock. It appeared to be blocked by some hard and gritty substance. What advice did I have?

Sharpe sprang immediately to mind. I asked the long-suffering Gibson for the morning off and went straight to the shop. Like Shelagh I found it impossible to insert the key. As far as I could tell, liquid cement had been squeezed into the lock to jam its mechanism. All I could do was find a locksmith to drill the lock out and fit another in its place. This he did and charged me heavily for his labours.

Certain only Sharpe could have done such a thing. I went to his house to confront him. Breathing fire as I was, it was perhaps as well that he was out for the day. At least so his wife told me before she slammed the door in my face.

My concern grew as I cooled down. If he was going to use the shop to gain his revenge for his lost court case, what would this mean for Shelagh who was going to be alone there every day? Could it put her in any kind of danger?

Shelagh, who was the bravest woman I have ever known, laughed at my fears when I expressed them that evening, but I knew I was going to live with the worry in the days ahead.

But the Record Shop had other enemies than Sharpe. On the very day we could not open it, Vee took our carefully worded advertisement to the local newspaper. She joined in the queue for paid inserts but when she reached the counter and handed hers in, the girl in attendance disappeared into a nearby office, only to return a couple of minutes later looking flustered. "I'm sorry but I can't take this."

Vee showed her surprise. "Why not?"

The girl hesitated, then said: "We're full for that night."

"Then put it in the following night," Vee told her.

The girl's embarrassment grew. "I'm sorry but I can't."

It proved to be true. The newspaper would not accept our advertisement. Des, Shelagh and I all tried at different times but in every case our submissions were rejected. We were denied entry into a public forum and there could be only one explanation. Big business had closed its ranks and was determined to deny us publicity.

I think it took us all a time to believe it. This was England in 1947. Des and I had gone to war in 1939 with fine-sounding phrases ringing in our ears. We were told the war was for justice, for the defence of the weak against the strong, for the sacred and inalienable rights of free speech and liberty. We were asked to put our lives on the line for these things and we had both volunteered accordingly. And what were we experiencing now? Had all those young friends we had known died for nothing? Had all that talk been pure cynicism?

I was embittered more than the others and I knew why. As a teenager I had witnessed my honest, hard-working mother lose her home, her possessions, and be put into the street through the scheming and cupidity of a wealthy businessman and such wounds are slow to heal, if indeed ever they do.

Then had come the war and after over four years abroad I had returned to England with such high hopes. But then had come the theft of my savings by colleagues, my encounter with the hatchet-faced landlady, my forced return to an office boy's job, the incorrect diagnosis about my heart, and then our encounter with Sharpe. All had created a sense of disillusionment but aware I was feeling sorry for myself I had fought it off so far by believing that sooner or later one's luck must change.

But it had not. It was happening yet again, but this time involving Shelagh directly. And Shelagh had given up so much for me.

The result of it all gave me a desire to start again. To begin life in another land. It was not a desire that came from Shelagh. She loved England and always said that none of our setbacks had turned her against it. But, almost without being consciously aware of it, I was beginning to want a total change of environment.

# TEN

In spite of the cold, the treacherous Press, and Sharpe, Shelagh still opened the shop. And to our surprise customers began to filter in and to take the odd record. Moreover, after a few days they increased in numbers. To our relief, they seemed to take reasonable care of the records. Encouraged, we felt that if we could only get publicity the project might still be a success.

My father gave us help here. Travelling round shops as he did, he suggested we had bills printed which he would ask shop managers to affix to their windows. Liking his suggestion, we used our first weeks takings to have some printed.

Our second week proved even more encouraging. Customers increased in numbers and those who had taken records began requesting more. Shelagh even managed to persuade two music lovers to hire our opera sets. Although we knew it was only early days, we began to feel that. in spite of its setbacks, the venture had a future and Des and Vee even discussed the possibility of opening a second shop elsewhere.

But towards the end of the second week I noticed Shelagh was unusually quiet after her return from the shop. When I questioned her she sat beside me and took one of my hands. "Darling, I've something I must ask you. Did you ever have a quarrel with Sharpe that you never told me about?"

I gave a start. "Whatever gave you that idea? No. The first one was when he insulted your mother. You know about all the others. Why?"

"I can't help wondering why he treats us this way. What have we ever done to him?"

"I've wondered myself. It can't be because of you. Perhaps it's what happened in the garden that day."

"But he was already doing those things. Even before mother arrived he was stealing our mail."

Her mood was puzzling me. "What is it, darling? Why are you talking about Sharpe tonight?"

Her hesitation told me it was something she didn't want me to hear and it took me a full minute to prize it from her. "It was what I found this morning when I opened the door. There was a large piece of burnt rag on the floor beneath the letter box and the inside of the door was blackened."

I gave a start. "You mean someone had tried to burn the place down."

She nodded. "That's what it looked like."

My feelings at that moment are better not printed. "Is that why you asked me if I'd had some secret quarrel with him?"

She did not deny it. Instead she gave a little sigh that affected me more than if she had broken into tears. "It's all such a shame, darling. I wanted so much for you to be happy. And I haven't brought you much luck yet, have I?"

I don't quite know why but those words brought back all the bitter memories mentioned in the previous chapter. And to make things worse she was blaming herself for them. My bitterness scalded me that evening. "Why on earth are you blaming yourself? I'm the one causing all the problems. I'm just so sorry it's all happening this way."

For the first time since our days in London I saw tears in her eyes. She reached forward and kissed me. "Stop worrying about it, darling. It'll all come right in the end."

My anger and frustration weren't so easily appeased. "I'm worried about you in that shop all day with Sharpe only a quarter of a mile away. I'm starting to wish I'd never thought of the damned idea."

"Stop worrying about me," she chastised. "Sharpe can't do anything in the daytime. In any case even he won't want to harm me physically."

I had never loved her and her courage more than at that moment. Seeing my expression she laughed and kissed me again. "Stop worrying, darling. Once this winter is over things will seem different again."

I could only hope she was right. Christmas came and went and yet the grip of that winter hardened. Because of the coal shortage the entire nation seemed to be either stumbling about in the dark or shivering in unheated rooms. Yet in spite of the conditions we managed to keep the shop open. Shelagh was the heroine, turning out every morning into conditions totally alien to her and shivering all day in the shop because of our inadequate fuel ration. One pitied the new government that had been elected in 1945. The tasks it faced seemed Himalayan.

There was also so much political bitterness. Half the country seemed resentful that Churchill, the architect of victory, had been unseated and Attlee put in his place as Prime Minister. Others, particularly ex-serviceman, were delighted at the change.

My personal feelings were mixed. On the one hand I admired Churchill and could well imagine his feelings at being ousted by the nation he had served so well. At the same time, unlike so many others who saw the nation as ungrateful, I saw the election in a very different light. By the time VE Day had arrived, Churchill's power had been greater than perhaps any Prime Minister in British history. The delegation of such power had been necessary for the successful outcome of the war but it was not a condition favoured by the British in peacetime.

As a consequence I didn't believe Churchill had been thrown out of government because he was unloved. On the contrary, I felt it was because he was loved too much. Some political instinct in the British has always made them chary of leaders whose charisma and power might make their position unassailable. Hadn't they just fought a war against a nation that, having allowed such a man to be their supreme leader, had paid a fearful price? While it is true that no two men other than Churchill and Hitler could have been more different, it is also true that power corrupts and a wise man bears that in mind.

To me, therefore, it was an instinctive, almost an atavistic suspicion of power that had made the British depose the man they loved. I believe Churchill himself saw this when his initial bitterness faded, for he had always believed political acumen was perhaps the greatest gift the British had given the world.

But, of course, there was much, much more to Churchill's demise. The war had been a massive leveller. Millions of young men, whose forefathers had taken for granted the superiority of the upper classes, had discovered in many foreign fields and in many crises that they were the equal or even the superior of the officers that commanded them. In addition the ABCA lectures they had been given throughout the war had tended to awaken in them an interest in politics, a subject their elementary school education had been careful to avoid.

Perhaps an even greater factor had been the liberation of women. Prior to the war a working class woman, struggling to clothe and feed her children on her husband's miserable wage, had found no time for dreams or ambition, nor had she related to the socialites and debutantes seen in the Picture Post or at the cinema. Envy didn't exist because envy needs a link of possible attainment, however tenuous. Such a link did not exist with those glamorous creatures from another world.

But the war had changed all that. Mobilized into nursing, or weapon production, working-class women had found themselves alongside socialites and debutantes and discovered to their surprise that they were not only as intelligent but their harsh backgrounds often gave them an edge over those who had known only wealth and privilege. Such revelations inevitably distorted the old political structure as men and women demanded a better deal for the sacrifices they had made.

Although my diary does record my thoughts on Churchill's fall, this is not to suggest I was overtly political at this time. But with the nation struggling to get back on its feet again and one's own life style and family affected by its progress, only a fool could avoid assessing the credits and debits of the two political parties. Mine was influenced at that time by a chance meeting I had with an old friend, Betty Simpson. Somehow — I never knew the details — Betty had become involved with the Communist Party during the war and said she had done some secretarial work for Harry Pollett, at that time the leader of the Party. As our meeting at the time coincided with the accession of Attlee and his Labour Party, I suggested the Communist Party must be pleased at the result.

Her smile betrayed my naiveté. Quite the reverse, she told me. Had I not noticed how since the war Communism had begun spreading across France?

"Yes," I told her. "That was why I thought your Party would be pleased. Doesn't this election make things easier for you?"

She shook her head. "It doesn't work that way. Causes prosper under adversity. If the Conservatives had won, ex-servicemen and the downtrodden masses would have flocked to us. As it is, the Socialists are giving people all we can give them, as well as leaving them with the franchise. So why should they come to us? It isn't just a body blow for the Party here. In turn it will affect the Party in France as well. Attlee is the worst thing that could have happened to Communism."

At the time I had no way of knowing if she was right. But history does record that after 1945 Communism was never a force of any consequence in England. And in France it retreated and mutated until it became little more than another minor political party.

Such were my political reflections and experiences in 1947. In our bread and butter life my concern was for Shelagh and the shop she was managing so well. By this time she had secured a number of regular customers and we all felt that when spring arrived the business would begin to show a reasonable profit.

However, I still could not get Sharpe out of my mind. He would be frustrated by seeing the shop's progress and would surely try some new ploy to damage it. But for what reason I kept asking myself. Why did he want to do us harm like this?

The answer came in a strange and moving way. One day in early January a girl in her early twenties crept into the shop with a parcel under her arm. Her voice was timid as if she were afraid of being overheard. "You are Mrs Smith, aren't you? The lady who used to live with Mr Sharpe and his wife?"

When Shelagh said she was, the girl handed her the parcel. "Then this is yours. I caught the postman this morning when he was about to leave it in the hall. I knew you wouldn't get it otherwise. He keeps everything of yours that still comes there."

Shelagh took the parcel. As she saw it was from her parents, the girl's voice broke in anxiously: "You won't say anything to Mr Sharpe, will you? Please don't. Things are bad enough already."

"When did you move in?" Shelagh asked.

The girl's eyes filled with tears. "Just before Christmas. We only got married six months ago and were so excited at finding a place. But it's awful. He's stealing our mail and writing dreadful things about us to our friends. And we've nowhere else to go. Arthur's parents are both dead and my Mum's been in hospital over a year. I don't know what we're going to do."

She had Shelagh's full attention by this time. "Have you or Arthur had a quarrel with him since you moved in?"

The girl shook her head. "No. That's what we can't understand. Why is he doing this to us? It doesn't make any sense."

"Go to the police," Shelagh urged. "Go to the police and we'll confirm your story."

The girl shrank away. "We can't do that. Arthur's out all day and I'm frightened what might happen. Don't say anything to anybody, please. Or I'll wish I'd never come over."

Shelagh tried to change her mind but it was no use. The girl hurried out of the shop and never returned. But that one visit explained all to us and relieved me from wondering if we were in some way the reason for our persecution.

The answer was simple and yet extraordinary. Sharpe was a psychopath who found pleasure in bringing misery to the young and the vulnerable, and the war had left him in an ideal position to indulge his perversion. While we had been his tenants and no others had been in his web, he had sated his lust on us. Now that two other victims had flown into it and were unable to escape, he was devoting his attention to them. In all likelihood we would be spared of him in the future.

Of course we should have gone to the police about him but as Des pointed out, what would we gain by it. We had no witnesses except Shelagh's father, and we could hardly expect him to make the long and expensive journey to England now that we no longer shared a house with the brute. We could only hope the young couple would soon find a way of escape as we had done.

Looking back at it from so many years later it seems odd that such behaviour had given us so much distress and worry. But like so many of us at that time, we had suffered from the war and longed for some security and happiness in our young lives. Because of this vulnerability, Sharpe had been able to indulge his perversion in ways that would have been more difficult in more peaceful years.

At the same time one is left with thoughts and questions that do little to support the faith and beliefs one was given as a child. Why had that one man, whose sole pleasure was to harm the young and vulnerable, survived the war when his neighbours and millions of others, a thousand times more qualified to live, had been killed? How does one dismiss a query that seems to question the very integrity of the world in which we live?

## ELEVEN

Spring came at last and with the malice of Sharpe having moved on I should have been more content. While not receiving any publicity other than our leaflets and customers' recommendations, the shop was paying its way and even giving the four of us a little pocket money over and above our salaries. Moreover, with Vee sometimes taking turns in the shop, Shelagh and I were now able to occasionally visit Hannah and William in Ruston Parva or take bus trips out to Bridlington and the Wolds. We even managed a weekend in Preswick where we visited my dear old Miss Kerr who had once been my host in my air gunner training days. I remember how her eyes had widened on seeing Shelagh and her whispered aside to me one day. "What a lovely girl, Frederick, and how beautifully she talks and behaves. Are you sure you will be able to hold on to her?"

I told her I would do my best and then took Shelagh to the Carrie hills and the Robbie Burns' cottage. She loved it all and we returned to Hull and my parents with happy memories.

But to my discredit I was still unsettled. I think the war was responsible. I had travelled the world never knowing what the next day would bring, and yet here I was spending my days sitting at a desk and doing a job I had done as a junior. I wanted something far better for both of us, something that would fulfil me and give Shelagh a less moody husband, and yet I could not identify its nature.

Although I did my best to hide this discontent, inevitably Shelagh sensed it. "What is it, darling? Have I disappointed you in some way?"

I was horrified that she should think that. "You? How can you think such a thing?"

"But there is something, isn't there? You're not truly happy, are you?"

"I'm not happy because I'm not giving you the life I want."

"But I'm happy enough. We're together again and we've got rid of Sharpe."

"I know that but you've still had to shiver in that shop all the winter. I was hoping by this time we could afford a manager. We probably could if that newspaper wasn't cheating us."

"Stop worrying about it," she told me. "We're together, we're in England, and its springtime. Think how lucky we are."

I knew she was right. And I knew she loved England. Then why the hell couldn't I make the best of things if only for her sake? I remember promising myself I would try.

It was the auction that exploded all my good intentions. Because the rooms in Sharpe's house had been large, we had been compelled to buy two pieces of furniture to fill them. One had been a large mahogany table and the other a non-utility sideboard that we had bought on credit for fifty pounds. Both were luxuries we could ill afford but the rooms needed them and at the time we believed the flat was our new home. But when Sharpe had driven us out, they proved too large for our new accommodation and for a while they had gone into storage. Now, tired of paying unnecessary fees, we decided to sell them.

So I phoned a nearby auction showroom to have the two pieces collected. With neither Shelagh nor I able to attend the auction because of work, I could only hope for the best when I went round to the showroom to collect the proceeds.

Even so I couldn't believe the money I received. It was one pound one shilling for the sideboard and seventeen shillings for the table! When I showed my incredulity the auctioneer shrugged his shoulders and told me the demand had been poor and if I wasn't satisfied, the fault was mine. I ought to have put a reserve price on both. When I told him I had known nothing about reserve prices, his shrug said it all. My ignorance was my fault, not his.

I was too stunned to argue. Yet as I walked from the showroom I still couldn't understand how both articles had awakened such little interest when the war had left such a demand for furniture. It was only when I was passing a large, second-hand furniture shop close by that I had the answer.

Both items were standing in the forefront of the window. The sideboard was priced at £61 and the table at £35. With no reserve to hinder him, the auctioneer and the second-hand dealer had done a deal between them.

I ran back to the auctioneer's shop, to find the man behind the counter had changed. It was now a beefy, rotund man with a florid face: a man whose face I remembered only too well.

It was the auctioneer who had been so brutal when taking away my mother's possessions after she had been driven into bankruptcy. The man who had behaved as if she had been a criminal instead of a victim.

I can't remember what I said to him. I only remember his words. If I was such a bloody fool not to put a reserve price on my goods, then what did I expect? It was business, wasn't it? Every man for himself. If I didn't like it, then I could fuck off and lick my wounds.

Mr Hyde had already been at the mouth of his cave on seeing the man. His language and insults were now all he needed. On the wall alongside me was a bayonet and scabbard. I remember some untouched cell of my mind thinking that characters like this make fat profits even out of war. But Hyde had no such abstract thoughts. He was single-minded. He grabbed the bayonet and then reached out and caught the man by his shirt collar.

Hyde's strength was frightening. The man was dragged over the counter and thrown down to the floor. Hyde dropped a knee on his belly and rammed the bayonet point at his throat. His voice wasn't mine. "So that's how business works, is it? You broke my mother's heart ten years ago and now you're trying to break mine. You thieving, corrupt bastard. I've killed better men than you."

I had never seen a man more scared. His eyes rolled and his cheeks went the colour of putty. How I got Hyde off him, I shall never know because I didn't want to. All the scars of my childhood were bleeding again and I wanted to kill him for opening them.

He saw it in my face and began pleading with me. I let him sweat for a minute, then drove the bayonet into the floor alongside him and walked out of the shop. I was trembling as I had trembled after my encounter with Sharpe, and perhaps for the first time in my life realized how deep the wounds of the past had been. At that moment I hated the society I lived in and wanted nothing more than to leave it.

It was without question an absurd reaction but the romantic in me had wanted so much to repay Shelagh for all she had sacrificed that perhaps I needed to lay the blame somewhere. During our long and painful separation I had thought of little else but of life with her in England and when fate had brought us together again life had seemed full of promise.

Instead everything had conspired against us, and in my embittered state I was starting to think our lives would remain star-crossed while we remained in England. To be fair to me I did have a physical inducement. Doctors had told me that my neck would benefit greatly if I went to a warmer climate (a prognosis that was to prove correct in subsequent years) but although the thought was there I can't say it was the main influence in my wish to emigrate. That was born entirely of secular events.

But of course there were problems. Apart from our commitments to Des and Vee, it was my parents that made me hesitate. They had given up their home for us for a property they had never wanted, and if we left them now, who knew what kind of tenants might move in with them? It all seemed a poor reward for their sacrifice.

I was also worried about their financial security. After their struggles and adversities both before and during the war, I had hoped for a better life for them but the only job my father had been able to get after their bankruptcy was menial, strenuous, and poorly paid. If I were six thousand miles away it would be impossible to monitor their circumstances.

In addition to all this, sentimental though it might sound, I had always been very close to them, and after our long separation I knew how saddened they would be if I left the country again.

As for the shop, we had made a commitment with Des and Vee and it didn't seem fair to break it at this time. So we soldiered on while the spring turned into summer. Although our limited budget and the newspaper embargo prevented our advertising the shop as we would have wished, word was slowly getting around and our clientele was growing. Our greatest thrill came when the Parks Department put in an order for records to play at their Sunday concerts. Although the total order only came to a few pounds, it made us feel we were breaking into the Big Time.

Nevertheless, our return was still pathetically small and as the weeks passed I think all four of us began to realize that without proper publicity we couldn't hope to have a flourishing business. The knowledge the 'Free Press' was the culprit did nothing to ease my general disillusionment and once again brought back the urge to move away and start a new life.

It was a quarrel at the Guildhall that brought things to a head. I've forgotten the precise details but a vacant post in a higher grade that I believed should be mine was given instead to one of the wartime temporary staff and I was left to continue sticking on my insurance stamps.

This happened the same week as we received notification that our 1946 application for emigration berths to South Africa had been accepted and we could sail the last week in August.

With emigrant berths to Commonwealth countries in huge demand, I knew this would probably be our only chance for years of obtaining one. I pointed this out to Shelagh who, in spite of having her son and family in South Africa, still loved England and in no way tried to influence me.

Yet the problem of leaving my parents behind still remained. Things might have been easier if my brother visited them more often, but when he did come up north he spent most of his time with our grandmother in Bridlington. The damage she had inflicted on our family had not healed with time, and the preference my brother showed for her was a permanent source of sorrow to both my parents.

Shelagh and I must have discussed the problem for days before we approached them. Would they consider following us if we emigrated? We knew it would be a huge step for them to take at their age but we would do all the spade work first and make sure of their comfort and safety once they arrived.

To my delight they agreed, although looking back now I'm convinced they did this only to ease our minds. Both were Yorkshire folk with their roots deep into northern soil, and neither could have fancied starting life afresh in a foreign land. My disillusionment after my homecoming had saddened them, and it was in their nature to put our interests before their own.

For me at the time, however, it was a huge stumbling block out of our way. Now we had only to obtain Des and Vee's blessing and we could be on our way.

This proved no problem at all. Both of them had been as disillusioned as I at the obstructions put in the way of an ex-servicemen's enterprise, and neither was interested in running the shop on their own. So it was amicably agreed that we should round up the business by selling our records.

We had no trouble putting this advertisement in the local newspaper. In fact it would probably have been accepted free of charge had we made the request. As the records were still in excellent condition, we decided to charge one shilling for each. At this price they went in large batches and by the first week in August we had sold over three thousand of them.

As we were obliged to give seven days notice on the shop, we stayed open one more week during which time we sold another three hundred of our remaining stocks at reduced prices. Of the rest, Des and Vee took any they wanted, and the rest we gave away to charities.

So our venture closed. As in the beginning we had only paid an average of sixpence for each record and as most had been on loan at least half a dozen times, it couldn't be said the project had been a failure even though it seemed everything had been stacked against it. The sale brought us in over £170 and our half was put towards the £112 we needed for our two fares.

The rest had to come from the sale of our home. This proved the easiest part of our move. The shortage of almost every household item in 1947 brought almost siege conditions to our flat after our advertisement appeared. People congregated on the pavement outside, queued up the stairs, and grabbed almost anything they could lay their hands on once they got inside the flat. Everything went, carpets, cushions, rugs, curtains: no matter how shabby, it sold. One felt the very wallpaper would have been stripped from the walls had it been detachable.

We sailed in late August from Southampton. The goodbyes had been painful and I didn't want to think about them. Yet our relationships with my family and friends and my meeting and marriage to Shelagh were the only memories of the last two years dear to me at that time. When I had sailed in wartime convoy in 1941, I had strained my eyes to see the last of my country. On this day, as the ship sailed into the Solent and then into the Channel, I don't believe I glanced back once. Such was my state of mind in 1947.

## TWELVE

Shelagh was four months pregnant when we sailed for South Africa. In her usual composed way, she had made nothing of it and had continued to look after our record shop, but with the winter weather and the rest of our misfortunes, it had been another factor that had made me feel we must escape before more happened to us.

However, those times were now in the past and after a few days at sea our youth and resilience took them from our minds. We were starting a new life and everything would be different in the future. We really ought to have known better but the Atlantic was blue, the bow waves white, and the sun was warm on our backs. We would not have been young if we had not been optimistic.

At the same time we were not on a pleasure cruise. Although classified as an emigrant vessel, our ship, used for troops during the war, had not been fully restored. This meant that although as emigrants we were paying the same for the journey as other passengers, we had only the same facilities as wartime servicemen. Thus while the women had cabins, we men, married or single, slept in dormitories of around forty others with canvas beds that were swung up and stacked away in daytime.

Nor did the similarities to war conditions end there. On being shown to my bunk by a steward, I was handed a broom. Asking what it was for, I was told it was to sweep my bed space in the morning and evenings. I would also have to take my turn in dishing out the food. The other men were given similar instructions.

I found this amusing. I might have still been naive in the ways of the business world but not in the wartime world that the stewards were trying to emulate. Paid to do the work, they were playing on the obedience of ex-servicemen and on the ignorance of those who were not. I handed my broom back to my steward with a few well-chosen words and to my satisfaction saw the rest of my dormitory begin to do the same. After that we had no further hassle.

To Shelagh and I these were small things that did little if anything to mar a pleasant journey. We had a day ashore in Madeira while the ship re-fuelled and took on supplies and then were off again.

Soon we were among the dolphins and the flying fish and they brought back memories of my first sea voyage, cramped on the deck at nights listening to the mournful cries of destroyers. At that time I had not known Shelagh existed, any more than I had known I would survive the war and one day be bringing her back on the same journey. When I gave the future thought, as I often did during that ten day journey, it seemed absurd to make plans. Life was too capricious to make speculation worthwhile.

Had I known it, I was experiencing a sample of life's vagaries at that very time. As the ship neared the tropics, I began to feel spasms of pain across the lower abdomen. At first they hardly bothered me but as the heat increased, they became more severe and once or twice doubled me up. As Shelagh was worried, I did as she asked and saw the ship's doctor. He gave me some mild sedative and the pain eased. I took this sedative until we left the tropics behind, when the pain eased and finally disappeared. With no reason to link the tropics with the discomfort, I assumed I had fully recovered.

Although as an emigrant myself I had little cause to be critical, I can't say that in general I was impressed by our fellow passengers. Everyone seemed to be moaning about Attlee's government and blaming it for the exigencies it had forced upon them, and how glad they were to be escaping from it. Considering the massive task it had to tackle, I found this criticism unfair and it further weighed the scales of my political sympathies.

Another topic of conversation was equally material: the better life they would soon be having in South Africa, the servants they would have, the extra possessions they would be able to afford. At one time I had seen emigration as a loss to the parent land. Now, as I listened to all this, I began to feel Britain was doing better out of this deal than was South Africa. Then I would come down to earth and ask myself what was I but another grumbler running away from post-war Britain? I found that thought disturbing.

We sighted Table Mountain in weather conditions exactly the same as they had been in 1941: in a storm force wind and driving rain. Yet the country had such happy memories for me that I stood on deck for hours watching the mountain drawing nearer. For

Shelagh the return must have had even greater significance because it meant she could see her son again. This thought must have been with her all the days and weeks I had dithered about emigrating, yet not once had she used it to influence me.

*Table Mountain, Clifton, South Africa*

But now she was back and her prospects must have been high when her parents and Monica met us at the docks and drove us to Clifton. The arrangements were that we could have a room in her parents' bungalow until I found a job and could afford accommodation of our own. One room was all we could be given because Monica was living in the bungalow at that time.

I find it hard to describe my feelings as the car swept round Bantry Bay and the four beaches and the twelve mountain peaks opened out ahead of us. I had fallen in love with Clifton six years ago and here I was back again. By this time the sky had cleared and the sun was flooding the mountains with light. Bungalows hugged the shallow cliffs alongside us and waves broke in clouds of spray on the four beaches. The air smelt of salt and pines and as I felt Shelagh's hand grip mine, I felt a deep sense of relief. We had done the right thing, I thought. In this beautiful land things must go right for us at last.

Our room was at one side of the bungalow and the rear window overlooked the sea to Camps Bay. It was true we had little space to set out the few things we had brought with us and these had to be stored below the bungalow. But this we expected and the beauty of the surroundings more than compensated for lack of space. At our first opportunity we walked to Big Rock on the end of the promontory and feasted our eyes on the soaring mountains, the white beaches, and Lion's Head. I had always thought Clifton the most beautiful place I had ever seen and after the trials of the last two years it seemed we had returned to paradise.

But we were soon to learn that even paradise cannot change the face of human nature. To record this is painful to me because the two people involved held, and still hold, my deep affection. Both had been kind to me in the past and were equally kind in the future. Moreover, both were victims of circumstances that can afflict anyone in their later years. I have to mention it because otherwise what follows would be meaningless, but I hope it will be done with sympathy and understanding.

Until then the novelty of our arrival had hidden from us a tension between Shelagh's parents or perhaps we had put it down to the general excitement of the occasion. But the atmosphere that evening when we all sat round the dinner table could have been cut with a knife. Distressed and puzzled by it, Shelagh asked Monica what was wrong and, after she gave us the details, her advice was that we should start looking for other accommodation right away. When Shelagh asked why, Monica explained that Pop seemed to be going through a mid-life crisis and the marriage was going through a rough patch. but that we would see for ourselves in a day or two.

I believe I was as distressed as Shelagh. Mac and Pop as they were affectionately called had stood by me during the war and taken care of Shelagh and her baby after my posting to the Far East. So I felt I owed them a great deal and it was painful to hear they were having marital difficulties.

We discovered the very next day that Monica wasn't exaggerating. Pop had been out into town and when he arrived back the two of them had a bad quarrel. To save everyone embarrassment, I walked down to Big Rock and waited half an hour before returning. When I entered our room Shelagh was looking pale and upset.

"Where are they now?" I asked.

She bit her lip. "Mom's gone for a walk and Pop's gone to see a friend. I don't know where Monica is."

"Did you say anything? Did you try to help?"

"Yes, but it didn't do any good." She put her head on my shoulder and I felt her tears on my cheek. "Monica's right, darling. Neither of us want to be drawn into it and have to take sides. The sooner we can afford our own accommodation the better."

I knew then that she had already been involved for trying to keep the peace. Without any security and with a baby only a few months away, we were in danger of becoming embroiled in a family quarrel only twenty-four hours after our arrival.

It was one of those situations when one does not know whether to laugh or cry. Certainly we were soon to realize that we had travelled six thousand miles only to fall from the frying pan into the fire again.

# THIRTEEN

I began looking for work the very next day. I combed the local newspapers, made phone calls, and wrote dozens of letters. I also made contact with Shelagh's brother Roderick, whom everyone called Boy. I had met him during the war when he was working as an electrician on the naval ships that docked in Cape Town for repairs. In build and character he was true to his Irish ancestry, a powerfully built, full-faced, ginger-headed man with an explosive temper.

On our arrival he would be about 38 years old and had his own small business in Mowbray, at the far side of Cape Town. It consisted of a shop on the main road where he displayed the electric motors that he re-wound, and a workshop thirty yards behind it down a narrow lane where the repair work was done. At this time he employed two men, a white apprentice and a black man called Rutherford. These two employees worked on damaged motors in the workshop and Boy shared his time between supervising their work and tending to the shop.

As he repaired motors for some large companies, I hoped he might know of some openings for me but here I was disappointed. The only openings he knew were for qualified electricians and at that time my knowledge of electricity was limited to the Rhumkorf Coil we had used at school.

In fact, as I combed the newspapers and trudged the streets, I became more and more conscious of my uselessness. Here I was, 28 years old, and my qualifications could be counted on two fingers. I was good at sticking on stamps (perhaps the best in the world at that) and no one knew more about guns, gunnery, bombs, and poison gas. In other words I was an expert on ways of killing people. Neither qualification was likely to send people screaming for my help unless I could foment a revolution. As the hot, dusty days passed I began to think I had emigrated to the wrong country. I ought to have chosen a banana republic.

By sophistry I did manage a few interviews but they all ended the same way. Except for one. It was with a petroleum firm — oddly enough the firm where Shelagh's ex-husband had worked before he moved up country with her son, Barry. On this occasion the office manager, a fast-talking character with glinty eyes behind horn-rimmed glasses, seemed quite keen to have me and when he took me to his place of work I understood why. His staff turnover must have been enormous because his glass-walled office was built on a kind of platform above a room filled with thirty or more desks. Men and women sat at these desks like rows of battery hens, all paging through piles of papers and scribbling information into ledgers. I was in the supervision office from which every move the workers made could be seen and analysed.

Leading me to the glass partition, Glinty-Eyes pointed down to an empty desk slap bang in the middle of the room. This desk could be mine if I were prepared to sign away my soul on the contract he offered me.

Even while he was talking, he never took his eyes off the battery hens below. Thinking about Shelagh and the baby we would have soon, I took the form from him. As I was reading it, he muttered something and reached out for a microphone on his desk. "Good morning, Mr. Miller. You're not looking too well this morning. Do we have a headache? If so and you come up to my office, I'll give you an aspirin."

I thought of myself sitting there day after day with Glinty-Eyes watching my every move, and my heart failed me. Shoving the unsigned paper back at him, I turned and fled.

Shelagh and I had one experience during this time that neither of us is likely to forget. Now that Shelagh was back in South Africa she had a legal right to see her son, Barry, and the boy was brought to us in September. He was a beautiful chubby child with fair skin and golden curls. In some mysterious way perhaps only women can understand, he attached himself to Shelagh as if she had mothered him all his life and he followed her everywhere. As I watched them and sometimes played with Barry myself, I remember praying that the baby Shelagh was soon to have would be a boy. Absurd though it was, I felt I would fail her otherwise.

So two happy weeks passed and then the boy had to go back to his father. I have forgotten who came to fetch him but I'll never forget that child's distress when he realised he was being taken away from Shelagh. He didn't just cry: he screamed as if his flesh were being torn from him.

I couldn't bear to watch Shelagh and went back into the bungalow. She looked half stunned and her lovely face was pale when she finally entered our room. When I tried to comfort her with some banal comment that it wouldn't be long before she could see the boy again, her reply shocked me.

"See him again! I'll never see him again. I've sent that message to Vincent."

I was aghast. "But why? The boy worships you. Didn't you hear how he cried?"

"Of course I heard. And do you think I'm going to let him suffer like that again? Just so I can be happy? I'll never do it to him again. Never, never, never!"

She never did. During the whole of our years in South Africa she never asked for another visit. I thought I had seen courage in my life but never courage of the kind Shelagh showed on that day of pain and loss. Such was the woman I had married.

It was Boy, her brother, who finally came to our rescue. Only a week after my arrival, discovering I had been a clerk in Local Government, he had asked if I would run over his books for him. It seemed he was concerned over the health of his business.

It hadn't taken me long to discover Boy's talents as an electrician did not match his office management. His books were atrociously kept, but even so it was clear he couldn't continue trading much longer without going into liquidation.

This puzzled me because, like almost every other country after the war, South Africa was run down on capital goods and so the repairing and re-winding of electric motors should have been a profitable business. It was Pop who solved the puzzle. Boy, he told me, was generous to a fault and customers traded on it. They would take motors on credit and then, to gain his sympathy, tell him some cock and bull story to avoid making payment later.

On checking his books again I found this was true. Had he insisted on prompt payments or demanded cash, he would have a healthy business. I told him that his friends were a liability and he must tighten up on them, and there I left it.

But he had not forgotten and after three weeks without my finding work he made me an offer. How would I like to take over the shop and the managerial side of the business while he devoted himself to the electrical side? If I agreed he would pay me £10 per week, the same wage he paid himself.

It was a generous offer but because I felt it was to help me I had to be equally certain his business could afford the additional expense. So, after talking it over with Shelagh, I took another look at his books. Certain now the credit factor was the key, I went back to Boy. "I'll do it but on one condition. You leave the entire sales side of the business to me."

He looked relieved. "Yes. That's what I want. You look after the shop and I'll repair the motors."

"You'll leave all the selling to me?" I insisted. "Even when your friends are involved?"

For a big man he had an endearing way of looking sheepish. "You think I'm too soft with them, don't you?"

"I know you're too soft with them. That's why you must let me handle them."

"You don't have to worry." he promised. "I shan't be in the shop, so you can do just as you like."

So we shook hands on it and early on Monday morning I made my way to the bus stop above 4th Beach. With the waves breaking below and the mountain peaks catching fire in the morning sunlight, I was reminded of the days in 1942 when I had risen early to make my way to the airfield. If anyone had told me that five years later I would be back there with a wife and a home, I would have laughed at them.

With the shop at Mowbray on the far side of Cape Town, it took two bus rides to reach it. Boy and his young wife, Pat, an English girl, were waiting there to show me the ropes. Until now Pat had helped with the secretarial work but with a child of four and another on the way, she was clearly pleased I was to take over. Before she left, with Boy safely away down the lane and out of earshot, she warned me about his good nature and how customers and friends played on it. "I've tried to stop him being so trusting but he takes no notice of me. In fact he loses his temper if people interfere. He even went for Pop when Pop told him he was too soft." She paused and eyed me. "You do know he's got an Irish temper, don't you?"

I was beginning to catch the drift of the conversation. "Shelagh has mentioned it once or twice."

"It's no problem with people he likes. But he doesn't take it well when people stand in his way. He hits out first and regrets it afterwards."

I was beginning to think I might earn my £10 per week. "I'm sure we'll be all right, Pat. He's assured me that I'll be in full charge of the sales side of the business."

"That's what he told me but it made no difference." Picking up her handbag, she paused, feeling perhaps that I needed reassurance. "Maybe you'll have more luck with him. Let's hope so or the business won't last much longer."

Her tone didn't suggest confidence of the highest order but I tried to reassure her that I would stand like a rock against any Boyish backsliding. After she left, I took stock of the shop again. It was of medium size with a counter, a chair, a typewriter, and a dozen or so electric motors of varying horse power exhibited in the windows or lying on the floor. A few ledgers and a few diagrams on the walls completed the picture.

With Pat's words warning me I had no time to waste, I found a piece of paper and scrawled across it in large capitals STRICTLY NO CREDIT GIVEN. This I pinned on the wall behind the counter and then occupied myself by designing a new method of accounts in the ledgers.

It was not long before my first test came. A large American car drew up outside the shop and a smooth-looking character with a military moustache and an English accent approached the counter.

"Good morning. Is Mr McGrath anywhere about?"

"He's busy at the moment," I told him. "Can I do anything for you?"

He eyed me up and down. "I haven't seen you before, have I?"

"No. I've just started here. What can I do for you?"

He eyed me again, then walked over to a 10 hp motor resting on the floor.

"That's mine. Boy's had it re-wound for me."

I examined the label. "Mr Scott?"

"That's right." He turned and waved forward a black man who was standing at the shop entrance. "Come and get this motor, Johnson."

I turned the label over where the price was marked. "I see Boy has the job marked at twenty pounds."

"That's OK," he said. "I'll see him later in the month." He pointed down at the motor to his servant. "That's the one. Stick it in the boot of the car."

Smiling my best smile, I stepped in front of Johnson. "I'm afraid I'm going to want the twenty pounds first, Mr Scott."

He stared at me as if I'd made an indecent suggestion. "What did you say?"

"I said I'll need paying for the motor before you take it away." I pointed at the notice over the counter. "We don't give credit here any more."

"Who says so?"

"I do."

"And who the hell are you?"

"I'm in charge of the shop."

"So that notice is your idea?"

"Not just mine. Mr McGrath has agreed to it as well."

For a moment he tried to humour me. "Look, I'm an old friend of Boy's. He'll give me credit. He always has."

"I know," I said. "To the tune of a hundred and fifteen pounds which you still haven't paid. I've seen the amount in the ledger."

His face darkened and he headed towards the door. "I want to see Boy."

I walked across and blocked the entrance. "Sorry but it'll make no difference. Do you want the motor or don't you?"

He looked as if he were going to try to push me out of the way. "I'm going down to the workshop. And you'll look a bloody fool when I come back."

I let him past me and waited. Five minutes later Boy and the two men entered the shop by the rear door. Boy's good-natured face showed embarrassment "Fred, you can let Scottie have the motor. He's one of the customers I always give credit to."

By this time I'd taken a dislike to Scottie. "I know you have. And he's also one of those who hasn't paid you for months."

A frown mingled with his embarrassment. "He's promised to pay in a couple of weeks when he expects a cheque from De Beers."

"Good," I said. "That's when he can have the motor, isn't it?"

At this Scott exploded. "Who is this bastard? Why the hell are you letting him treat your customers this way?"

It was a remark meant to incite Boy and it had its effect. "He's new here, Scottie, and doesn't know who my friends are yet. You can have the motor. But try to pay me at the month end."

It needed nothing more than Scott's triumphant look to fire my Mr Hyde. "What about the deal we made? Don't you keep your promises?"

It wasn't the most tactful thing to say. I'll swear his ginger hair stood on end. "I've never broken a promise in my life."

"You're breaking one now if you give him that motor. You gave me a free hand and now you're tying my hands behind my back. Can't you see it's crooks like this who're destroying your business? He's not your friend. He's a bloody con man."

I could have been more tactful. As Boy's face went red and his big fists clenched, I felt I'd struck a detonator with a hammer. For a long moment family harmony looked like exploding into a hundred fragments. Then he muttered something and turned to the incensed Scott. "I'm sorry, Scottie, but I did make him the promise. You'll have to pay for the motor now if you want to take it away. Sorry, but you see how it is."

Heated comments followed but they ended with Scott snarling

something to his servant and then storming out of the shop. As the two of them drove away, Boy gave me a look and without another word disappeared through the rear door. I sank into a chair telling myself I should have taken Pat's warning. There was no way I could work with a man like this.

I should have known better. Once Boy's Irish temper subsided, there wasn't an ounce of malice left in him. He returned to the shop at lunchtime and held out his hand. "I'm sorry. You were right all the way. Come and let me buy you lunch."

I'm not saying we never had another quarrel. We had plenty in the days that followed but they all ended with a handshake. As our respect for one another grew, so did the business. Once convinced I was right about the cash guidelines, Boy suggested we formed a private company and generously insisted I became an equal partner.

So by the time Christmas 1947 came, although we had not been able to find alternative accommodation, it did begin to look as if some aspects of our lives were beginning to fall into place. After all that had happened so far, we really should have known better.

# FOURTEEN

It is often said that problems seldom come singly and it was certainly true of us in 1948. And yet the year began on a happy note. During the last days of her pregnancy, with the total lack of fuss or bother that was Shelagh's way, she went into the Inverugie hospital in Seapoint and on the 3rd January our first child was born. To my immense relief it was the boy I had prayed for. We christened him Peter Raymond. The second name, Raymond, was Shelagh's choice. She felt it would please my brother.

However, delighted as we both were, the needs of a baby did not make our living in one room and in an unhappy bungalow any easier. To make things worse, earlier that month Monica had married and until she and her husband could find accommodation they were sharing Monica's room. So we were all squeezed together like sardines in a tin, with all the explosive pressures such situations create.

As a consequence, in spite of Shelagh's initial delight at having Peter and in spite of her tolerance and courage, there were times in the weeks that followed when I found her in tears when I returned home. Worried about her, I tried even harder to find a flat but still without success. Some of the blame for this had to be laid at the door of South Africa House in London. Had we been warned earlier that South Africa was suffering the same housing shortage as England, it is possible we might not have gone there. Certainly I wouldn't have made the promise to my parents that I would bring them over once I'd found a job. If we couldn't escape from one room, what hope was there of finding a home for them?

I found it all very depressing and as the tension in the bungalow grew, there were times when even the days with Sharpe seemed almost tolerable.

To complicate things Boy and I had trouble with the police that year. Rutherford, our black electrician, was an expert at re-winding motors and, according to Boy, could rewind a car armature or refrigerator motor in fifteen minutes or less. As much of our work came from such repairs, he was an invaluable member of the staff

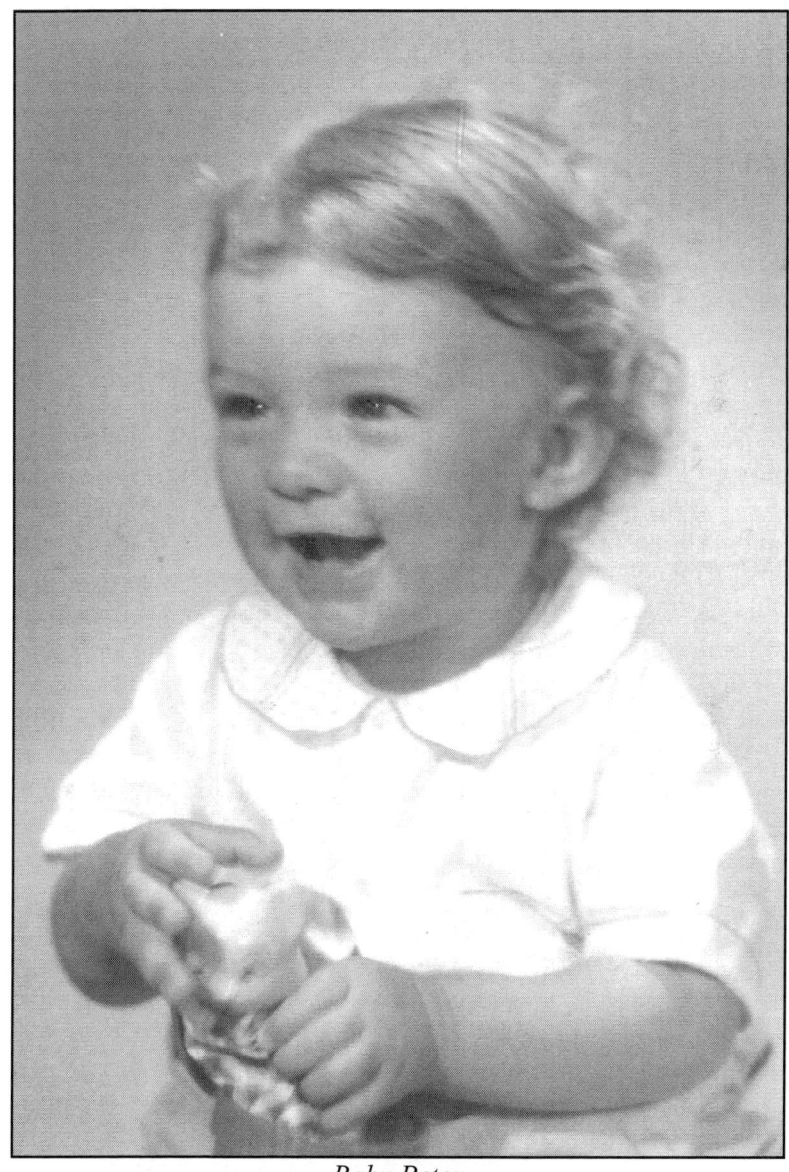
*Baby Peter*

and so we paid him the same wages as we paid ourselves.

In doing this, however, we were breaking the law. Legally no black man was allowed to do skilled or even semi-skilled work. Both Boy and I found this blatant hypocrisy because we sometimes rewound motors for large companies like De Beers, and on our visits we often saw black workers doing skilled work. It was even said De Beers used them as diamond cutters while at the same time paying them a labourer's wage.

Although I never witnessed this personally, it wouldn't have surprised me because by this time I had realized there was one law for the companies whose massive profits aided Government finances and another for tiny private companies like our own. So we quite shamelessly let Rutherford do what he was good at doing and paid him accordingly.

But in late January a police car turned down our lane and a few minutes later Boy and two policemen entered the rear door of the shop. It seemed an onlooker had seen Rutherford working on a motor and had reported it to the police.

I could tell from Boy's expression that we were in serious trouble because he was not one to cry wolf lightly. For my part I was tempted to say that South Africa needed all the skilled technicians she could get and it was prejudiced nonsense to deny a man skilled work because of his colour.

But with two scowling policemen looking as if they were about to arrest us at any moment, it was not the time to voice such comments. So instead I put on my most innocent face and, pretending I was the one responsible, said I'd only been in the country a short time and hadn't realized we were doing anything wrong.

I felt both a coward and a hypocrite but there seemed no other way of saving Boy's business. After a long conference in Afrikaans, the policemen told us no charge would be preferred this time. But if in the future Rutherford did anything other than strip the old wire from the motors and acted as a cleaner, we would be for the high drop. The looks they gave us before leaving made it clear they would be keeping a close eye on us in the future.

We were left wondering what to do with Rutherford. We could hardly pay him the same wage to do only menial work and yet knew the hardship a huge drop in wages would cause his family. Finally we compromised by offering him eight pounds a week until he found another job that paid as well. We knew this was highly unlikely but Rutherford was a decent man and we were grateful for the work he had done for us.

Because this offer was a drain on the business, we let him rewind motors occasionally while keeping him out of sight of prying neighbours. As this was a strain on our nerves, it was a relief when he finally obtained a job with a local steel firm. His wage, he told us, would be only four pounds a week but he felt he could no longer burden us with a wage he wasn't earning. Such was the integrity and quality of the man the State did not regard as equal to its white citizens.

As if we were not having enough problems during this time, I compounded them by agreeing to play in a football match organised by a friend living nearby. It was stupid of me because after the knee accident that had lost me an athletic career, I had been warned never to play the game again. But as I was now playing tennis without any problems I decided the knee was fully cured.

I was soon proven wrong. When taking a shot at goal an agonising pain shot through the knee. Down I went and had to be carried off the field

I had to be driven home after the match. Because Boy and I had only just formed our private company and I knew how much he needed me in the shop, I was furious with myself. How without a car was I going to get to work?

I phoned Boy and explained my situation. Being Boy, he laughed at my concern. I must stay at home until my leg was better. He would manage perfectly well, so I mustn't worry.

It wasn't that simple. Lying in the congested bungalow I could not help seeing how difficult things were for Shelagh with her baby, and how often she was drawn into arguments and situations that were no fault of her own. Making matters worse by defending her, I soon decided it would be better for Shelagh, indeed for everyone, if I went back to work

So on the third day, against Shelagh's wishes and with a knee still as large as a grapefruit, I made an attempt to reach the bus stop at the top of the promontory. With no crutch and only a stick as support, I would have had problems had not Maggie offered to help me.

Maggie was a sixteen year old black maid Mrs Mac had taken on soon after our arrival from England. Maggie had everything: a huge watermelon smile, two rows of strong white teeth, a head of curly black ringlets, and a body as strong as a bull elephant.

The white kids loved her. No matter how hard a day's work she put in, Maggie was always ready for a game with them. I never saw her frown or heard her complain. Maggie seemed to lack all the mean, envious, and malicious elements that so often disfigure the rest of us.

Indeed I think Maggie was the reason I came to like black people. Maggie was so generous. Generous with her smile, generous with her work, generous with everything, including her body. She had a small room below the bungalow where she sometimes entertained her boy friends. Maggie loved life and so she loved men too.

The only people who disapproved of Maggie were Clifton's virtuous matrons. The rest of us, including Mrs Mac, thought the world of her.

To my credit Maggie saw me as a friend. Even prior to my accident she would go out of her way to do little jobs and errands for me. Now that I was lame, she was in her element. There was no need for Shelagh to meet me at the bus stop and help me down to the bungalow. When six o'clock struck Maggie would drop everything and run up the road to collect me.

It wasn't then a question of my putting an arm round her broad shoulders and letting her take some of my weight. That sissy stuff was for the whites. Maggie would sling me, a thirteen stone man, halfway across her back and nearly carry me down the road. It was no use my objecting: she did it anyway. She would lower me down at the top of the little flight of steps outside the bungalow door, give me that big warm smile of hers, and then go down to her little room.

Maggie was someone you can never forget. Maggie was a beautiful human being.

It took well over a month before I could walk reasonably well again and after experiencing Shelagh's problems in the bungalow I was determined to find other accommodation or die in the attempt. So in every moment of my spare time I searched Cape Town for a flat or even a room where we could live in tranquillity again. I did find one or two vacant flats but they were far too expensive for us.

It was during one of these forays that I had an unforgettable experience. I had seen a flat advertised in the Press and although from its location I knew the rent would be excessive, desperation makes its own priorities and I went to view it

It was sited in a large expensive complex on the lower slopes of the city. Coming out of the lift I saw three other flats shared the same floor. As I made towards the one advertised I heard a door close behind me. Glancing over my shoulder, I saw a slim, elegant blonde woman making her way towards the lift. I stared at her, unable to believe my eyes. "Synneva! It is you, isn't it?"

She turned. At first she did not recognise me. Then her eyes suddenly widened. "Frederick! Oh, my God."

I couldn't believe what I was seeing. "Do you live here now? Have you left Oranjezacht?"

Her mind was not on my question. "Frederick! I can't believe it. I thought you were dead."

I hardly knew what I was saying myself. "Why did you think that?"

"Someone told me you'd been sent to the Far East. And when I never heard from you again I thought . . . ." She broke off, then motioned to the door of her flat. "Come inside, please."

It was a flat like the one she had owned before: expensive and tastefully furnished with her paintings around the walls, a flat that expressed everything she was. Her expensive perfume drifted my way as she motioned me to sit down. Still half-stunned by the encounter, I hardly knew what I was saying. "Why did you move flats?"

She looked equally spellbound by our encounter. "The lease expired but in any case Bjorn had bought this block and so it seemed only good sense to move into it."

"Then you're still married to Bjorn?"

"Oh, yes. I always will be. We're too good friends ever to separate. But what about you? Are you married?"

"Yes. To Shelagh. A South African girl I met before my posting."

"Did you marry her then or after the war?"

"After."

"I see. So that is why you're back in South Africa?"

"In a way yes. I suppose it is."

It was like being transported back in time as we talked. I could see no change in her. She looked as elegant as the day I had first met her on Clifton Beach. I can't remember what else we said. It was like some strange dream of the past. I have no idea how long we talked but at last she glanced at her watch and gave a start. "How quickly time goes. I'll have to be on my way."

*Synneva*

I wondered who her new lover was. She would not be Synneva without one. I went to the lift with her. There she glanced at the door of the vacant flat. Do you think you will take it?"

I had already made my decision and shook my head. "No. I've decided it will be too expensive for us."

Our eyes met and then she gave me a little understanding smile. A moment later she kissed my cheek. I took her slim hand that I had held a hundred times before and lifted it to my lips. A little sob broke from her. Then the lift came and with a last glance at me she stepped into it and was gone. It was the last time I ever saw her.

Although I was now mobile again and my neck problems were much better in the warmer climate, that same climate brought back the second illness the war had inflicted on me. As summer advanced I had a re-occurrence of the bowel pains I had felt on the ship. They became worse as the temperature rose and Shelagh wanted me to seek medical attention. But there was no NHS in South Africa and as doctors' fees were expensive I managed to survive the rest of the year without calling on one.

But the pain hardly eased that winter and when summer returned they became so severe that I was forced to seek help. Unable to identify the illness, my doctor gave me the recently discovered drug penicillin and for a couple of weeks the pain eased. When it returned he plied me with pills and potions until they almost came out of my ears, and when none worked and I began losing weight he insisted I went into hospital for a detailed investigation.

Although once again I didn't want to leave Boy to handle the shop alone, the pains now gave me little choice. Fortunately the young doctor I saw this time possessed a brain as well as a stethoscope, and after I told him how the pains were always worse in heat, he gave me a stool test.

The result came a week later. I was suffering from chronic amoebic dysentery, almost certainly contracted during my war service in the Far East. The reason I had avoided symptoms in England was because the cooler climate had sent the amoeba into a kind of hibernation. In the warmer climate of the Cape they were active again and if I were to escape liver damage and other unpleasant effects, I must have treatment at once.

Dismayed, I asked if I could be an out patient and continue to work. The answer was an emphatic no. The drug emetin I would receive was severe in its effects and a patient must be strictly immobilized. The only bright spot of this dismal forecast was that I could be given the drug at home if I promised to behave myself and not leave my bed. In all, the treatment would last around seventeen days.

Thinking about Shelagh and the difficulty she would have in visiting the hospital, I opted for home treatment. In the circumstances I should have known better but by this time the pains were so severe I wasn't able to think clearly.

Boy, as always, was generous to a fault. "The main thing is to get yourself better. Don't worry about me. I want you for the years ahead. I've managed before and I'll manage again."

I couldn't do this to him. I had been warned that I wouldn't be allowed to work for weeks after my treatment, and as our business had trebled in the last year, Boy would never be able to manage both the shop and the workshop. This left me with no alternative but to get him another partner. I talked it over with Shelagh and we both decided the fairest thing to do was to sell my share of the business.

Boy fought us all the way, generously arguing that I had transformed the business and it wasn't right I should lose my share of it when the rewards were beginning to come in.

I wasn't so noble that I didn't have the same regrets myself. Although he had played his full part in our recovery, I had worked very hard and it did seem cruel to go back to the hard old days again. Perhaps I might have behaved differently with another partner but when a man plays as fair as Boy, how can one let him suffer for it?

The problem was finding him a partner he could work with and who would be useful to him. He knew plenty of electricians but most of them hadn't two pennies to rub together. On the other hand there were plenty of oily characters who were willing enough to buy into businesses of this kind and take the profits without working for them.

The outcome was what I expected it would be. An electrician Boy liked offered us £500, less than half an offer we had already been made and one that only covered the basic cost of the shares I'd bought. Boy didn't put the slightest pressure on us but I could guess what he was hoping. I talked it over with Shelagh and we decided to accept the electrician's bid. When we looked at one another that night, we knew we really were back to square one again.

So the course of treatment could now begin. I little knew of the problems it would cause.

## FIFTEEN

I began my treatment in the bungalow a few days later. The emetin was to be injected intravenously once a day by my GP. He was one of the ex-patriots who had fled from England when the Labour Government had introduced the Health Service, and from the useless pills and potions he had given me, I had already realized that he knew next to nothing about tropical diseases.

However, he could talk and handle a syringe and that was all required of him. Ordering me into bed, he passed on the Hospital's instructions. I must lie as still as possible for the next seventeen days. This was because emetin weakened the heart muscles and even the movement of my arms could be dangerous. For the same reason I must indulge in no exercise whatever for at least three weeks after the end of the treatment to allow my heart to recover. With that he squeezed what seemed like half a pint of brown liquid into my arm and departed.

I lay with my thoughts and it isn't difficult to guess their nature. My heart specialist in Hull had scoffed at the earlier diagnosis of two doctors and given me a clean bill of health. At the same time he had warned me their opinions would almost certainly have left me with a psychological scar and the day would come when I might question his judgement against theirs.

But even he had never anticipated a situation as ironical as this. Here I was, lying helpless in bed, being given a drug that on medical admission would progressively weaken my heart. What if my specialist was wrong or even half wrong? What would happen before the treatment ended?

Commonsense told me that as I had already lived two years and not spared myself, my heart must be sound. But when does common sense enter into an equation of this kind? As each day passed and more emetin was pumped into me, I had a recurrence of the old symptoms. I would hear my heart thudding in my ears and feel it straining in my chest. With little faith in doctors by this time, I began to believe emetin was killing me.

With his profession to blame, one would have thought my doctor would have shown some understanding and patience with my apprehension. Instead he dismissed it in a way that made me feel unable to mention it again.

So, with Shelagh nursing me and trying to look after the baby at the same time, a week passed. During this time Monica and her husband obtained rooms from a friend and moved from the bungalow. As a consequence Mrs Mac told Shelagh she would like me to move into their old room and take some of our furniture with me.

Knowing the danger, Shelagh made an immediate protest. I would move as soon as the doctor gave me permission, she said. At the moment it was too dangerous. But Mrs Mac would have none of it. Now that Monica had gone she wanted the bungalow re-arranged.

I have no wish to blame her for her reaction. She was on the edge of a nervous breakdown and I am certain she did not understand the risks involved. On the other hand I could not lie there and allow Shelagh to suffer daily quarrels with her either.

So one day the fractious part of me that takes over when I am frustrated could stand it no longer. Damning the consequences I rose from my bed in spite of Shelagh's frantic protests and dragged the named pieces of furniture into the other room. Then I dropped on the new bed and fought for breath.

It was beyond any doubt a stupid thing to do because when my temper returned I knew full well that Mrs Mac had meant no harm to me. Proof of this came later when she entered the room and asked my forgiveness. Giving this to her was no problem but it was less easy to forgive myself. I lay there wondering if my temper and impulsiveness had done my heart irreparable damage.

Nor did the doctor's arrival bring any comfort. After he found I was in a different bedroom, I heard him remonstrating with Shelagh and her mother. Why had they allowed me to move? Had he not warned us all? Didn't anyone understand the dangers involved?

He was in no better mood when he came in to see me. After he checked my heart and I asked its condition, he gave only a non-committal grunt, no doubt to punish me for my transgression. He then gave me another shot of emetin, asked me sarcastically which room I'd be in on his next visit, and departed.

With everyone shaken up by the incident, the treatment was completed without any further stresses. I was eventually allowed out of bed but told to take things very easy for another three weeks. I enquired how my heart had come out of the experience and was told I had nothing to worry about if I did as I was told and took no exercise of any kind.

But psychological scars are not so easily assuaged. With our future insecure again, I had to know I was well and strong enough to face it. So on the third week, without telling anyone, I climbed up the mountain as far as the Cable Station. When I reached it without dropping dead, my faith in my Hull specialist returned.

Yet although no harm came to me, I site this impulsive act as a reminder to doctors that they have the power to harm us as well as heal. Perhaps to avoid such mistakes, a new approach to medicine could be devised. As the diagnosis of some illnesses can be more difficult than the curing of them and so might require investigative skills as well as medical knowledge, would it not be a good idea to have diagnostic centres in all towns and villages in which such specialists are housed? Then, with their diseases properly identified, patients could progress to the rank and file GPs who would now have no problem in giving the correct treatment or issuing the right prescriptions. In this way much time, money, and personal distress might be saved.

As the hospital had decided my amoebic dysentery had been contracted during the war, I was advised to apply for a military pension. This I did and after much ado was awarded sixteen shillings a week. Although little enough, it was still a help to us because, since my amoeba problem had been diagnosed, medical expenses had been taking over 25% of my salary. Nevertheless, with my mother's past example in mind, I had suggested to Shelagh that we put the five hundred pounds from the share sale into a contingency fund. It was the only security we had, and the way our luck was running we might find ourselves in an even worse situation than at the moment. She agreed and the bulk of the money was banked on the understanding it would only be plundered in the direst emergency. The balance we kept was to carry us through until my convalescence was over and I could find another job.

As it turned out, we didn't need the money. Mrs Mac would take no rent or money for food from us during that time, proving if proof were needed that her recent irascibility was due to health factors over which she had no control.

Fortunately the task of finding a job also proved easier this time. Mrs Nolan, a neighbour who worked as a clerk in a firm manufacturing gates and wire fencing, offered to speak to the secretary. He interviewed me and as a result I was offered a job in the main office as the second-in-charge clerk.

My heart sank at the thought of office work again, but beggars couldn't be choosers and I reported for work the following Monday at the firm's factory in Woodstock on a salary of £35 per month.

It couldn't be called a salubrious site. Woodstock, lying below Devil's Peak, was on the fringes of the infamous District Six where it was said the police were hesitant to enter. The factory lay halfway up a shallow hill with a small park opposite. The offices were in an adjoining building, the main office on the upper floor and below it other smaller ones that housed the directors, the secretary, and other clerks and typists. Our office, which mostly handled the accounts, had six members at that time: a nervous man in his late thirties named Russell who was in charge, Mrs Nolan, three other female clerks and myself. My tasks were to cost the jobs that the salesmen obtained and to produce a balance sheet every month of one of the smaller commercial enterprises owned by the parent firm. I was also to learn Russell's job so I could step into it when he went on holiday or if he fell ill.

I had only been working there two days when I ran into a small neat man in his mid forties coming out of an office. He stared at me, moved away a few paces, then turned. "Don't I know you?"

"I'm new here," I told him. "I only began work on Monday."

"Yes, but I've seen you somewhere before. You're English, aren't you?"

"Yes. I came over here in '47."

He drew closer. "Were you in the RAF?"

"Yes. I served in England until the middle of '41 and was then posted overseas."

He gave a sudden laugh and held out his hand. "Then you're Smith. We were on the same station in East Anglia. Don't you remember? I was the Belgium engineering officer. Now I'm one of the directors here."

To be honest I couldn't remember him at all although I didn't say so. He drew me into his office and made a great fuss of me. "You did a fine job there, Smith. I've never forgotten it."

It brought back to me the way the CO had treated me in 1941 after I had received my head and neck injury. What notable deed had I done to earn their praise, I wondered? If it had been anything worthwhile it must have been done while I was still concussed because I had no memory of doing anything else other than my routine duties.

However, with the instinct of a survivor and at the risk of sounding disingenuous, I felt it unwise to pursue the point further, particularly as it had a director's approval. So I left it there and had reason to be grateful for my prudence in the days that followed.

## SIXTEEN

As I had never liked office work, I had not expected to enjoy the days ahead but what I hadn't known was that Russell was a desperately insecure man who lived in constant fear of being upstaged or even supplanted by those beneath him. As I was the one scheduled to learn his job, and as my history of English Local Government Service seemed to impress him, I became the target of his fears.

If the poor man had only known it, he could hardly have been safer. Double entry bookkeeping, balance sheets and the rest of the rigmarole had remained mysteries to me ever since 1937/8 when I had cycled to night classes three evenings a week in futile efforts to understand them. If he had attempted to teach me his job in entirety, he would probably have failed.

As it was I had no chance of failure because he had no intention of teaching me anything. He would feed me little snippets of information that out of context were dangerous rather than helpful, and side track me whenever I sought to know more about the tasks I was supposed to learn.

As my main job was costing accounts, this hardly mattered during the first few weeks. Armed with a Walther Accounting Machine, and learning pence to six decimal points, I could rattle off costings at great speed. My problems arrived when his holidays became due. How could I stand in for him when I had no idea what would be asked of me?

Fortunately he took his holidays only in short spells that year. He gave his reasons as domestic — he and his wife had decided to spend his holidays working on the house — but I'm certain I was the cause.

Not that I had any complaints. I began wishing he would never take holidays. No one likes to split on a colleague, even when they're being deliberately obstructive, but equally I didn't want the secretary to think I was a 'thickie'. I had, after all, a wife and child to support.

With this in mind, I kept asking Russell when he was going to teach me enough about his job to hold the fort while he was away. I inferred that was all I needed. When he still kept on prevaricating, my temper began to fray. I pointed out that on at least half a dozen occasions I had been asked by the secretary for information I couldn't provide because of his bloody-mindedness. If he didn't come clean, I would be forced to tell the truth. I was no longer prepared to let the secretary think I was a fool and risk losing my job in the process.

He denied everything and then continued in the same vein until the day came when I was asked for figures I couldn't provide and it all came spilling out. The secretary admitted Russell could be difficult but went on to tell me that he was very good at his job. When I asked why he had to treat it like the Holy Grail, he tapped a pencil on his desk for a moment, then seemed to come to a decision. "Don't worry about it. You carry on with your costings and I'll find you some other job if you've any spare time over. That way the two of you won't clash again."

I wanted to ask why Russell was allowed to get away with this extraordinary behaviour but had the feeling it would be a waste of time. I also wondered why I was being kept on if from now on I was only to be a kind of odd jobs man. Had my Belgium director given orders I should be retained at all costs, I wondered.

Then I shrugged and went back upstairs. At least I wouldn't have to worry about balance sheets and cash flows any longer. On the other hand, as I could hardly be considered second in charge if I couldn't step into Russell's shoes, had my chances of promotion just taken a steep dive into nowhere? Time was to prove me correct.

In all I was to have nearly three years in that office and they weren't by any stretch of the imagination the happiest of my working years. I have always found offices tend to be hotbeds of malice, perhaps because human beings aren't meant to be confined together between four walls for months and years on end. Nevertheless there are offices and offices, and ours was rent by petty quarrels that often seemed to have no real substance.

The problem lay in weak leadership. The war had taught me that men and women work best when their orders are firm and unequivocal. In this office the reverse was true and so petty quarrels were almost a daily occurrence.

It was a depressing ambience and I began to dread the mornings when I had to leave the beauties of Clifton and make my way to that hot and clattering factory. As the months passed by I felt I was building up a numbing wall round myself, a self-protective defence against the boredom of my work.

An incident one afternoon epitomised these feelings. I had been out to post a parcel and as I was seldom out of the office during working hours I had spent as long as possible over the task. As I walked back to work I saw a flight of doves flying back and forth against the green beauty of Devil's Peak. As I watched them, a sudden envy caught my breath. If it were not for Shelagh and the baby, and some higher power had offered me an exchange into those small white bodies I would have accepted it with joy. What had we done to our lives to wear such chains when other living creatures could still know freedom? My envy was exquisite as I watched those birds diving and swooping in the bright sunlight.

To be fair to that office and its inmates, the conditions didn't help. The low corrugated iron roof under which we worked turned it into a broiling room in the summer months of January and February. Various stratagems were tried. Huge blocks of ice were brought in and fans set up behind them but the temperature was never lowered more than a degree or two. On a few occasions the women were sent home and the men left to sweat it out. I have vivid memories of tottering into the nearest pub at five thirty and downing pint after pint of lager to counteract the dehydration.

It was at this time that I had one of the strangest experiences of my life. Because of the impression the old Yogi had made on me during my service days in India, I had continued doing the physical and mental disciplines he had shown me and I had made considerable progress. I had mastered all the physical and breathing exercises, could increase or decrease the pace of my heart by concentration, and, most difficult of all, had trained my body to relax at will.

This last discipline proved its great usefulness during these office years. Returning home full of frustration after yet another encounter with Russell, I would lie down on the floor of our bedroom and try to eliminate all the tension from my mind and body. The floor was necessary because otherwise muscles would tense as the surface yielded under one's weight.

*Myself practising yoga*

The secret was to perfect the discipline until muscles as tiny as those of the skin relaxed, giving the feeling the very skin and flesh were turned to liquid and running from one. To achieve such control can take a long time and until now I'd never reached this state of perfection.

But on this one special night I succeeded. As one muscle after the other surrendered its sovereignty, my body seemed to lighten until it was no longer the clay that tied it to the earth. Soon it was so light I was once again the child who had imagined himself swimming with the fish among sunlit rocks and reeds. It was a blissful feeling and I did not want to awaken from it.

But then the image shattered. Suddenly I found myself in space and gazing down at my bedroom floor on which a body was lying. It was my body and fear suddenly gripped me. Somehow I had broken the chain of contact that linked us together. Surely I would die unless I could return. Perhaps I was already dead and beyond salvation!

Panic broke the spell. In a flash I was back on the floor with my heart racing and my body sweating. When Shelagh entered the room shortly afterwards, she said I looked as if I'd seen a ghost. At the time I felt I had. My own ghost.

For years I puzzled about that experience. During my days in Quetta my Indian yogi had told me I would progress far along the path of enlightenment if I continued to practise the art, but had also warned me that because of my western upbringing the time would come when fear would call a halt to my progress. Somewhat incredibly, he had prophesied this moment, the one when I achieved the severance between the mind and body.

I told myself his prophecy had been lying unsuspected in my mind all this time and so because of the tensions of the day it had emerged as a dream. I think I convinced myself of this because otherwise the implications were too disturbing.

I might have gone along this way for the rest of my life had I not met a woman some years later who was a member of a novel writing course I was tutoring. At lunchtime our conversation had somehow come round to Yoga and I told her about this experience. When I expressed my scepticism and said it had only been a dream she shook her head. No, it had been no dream, she assured me. She knew this from something that had happened to her.

I listened with fascination to her story. She had not been practicing Yoga nor even thinking about it at the time. She had been out for a walk one summer afternoon in Devon and found herself on a minor road she had not seen before. A hundred yards ahead the road swung to the right but she could not see any further because of the high hedges on either side. As she walked towards the bend she had a sudden feeling of disorientation and a moment later found 'herself' thirty or forty feet above the road and looking down at herself below. At this point she gave an embarrassed laugh. "I know it sounds crazy but my body was still walking. And yet I was suspended above it like a fluttering bird."

"Could you see anything of your new self?" (I asked this because I had seen nothing of myself when in this strange mode).

She shook her head. "No. But the entire countryside was spread out below and it seemed to be rising and falling as if the earth itself were breathing."

"Did you get a fright the way I did?" I asked.

"Not immediately. But then it occurred to me I must be dead and I became terrified. That was when I found myself back in my body again."

Fascinated though I was, I still couldn't see how any of this was proving I hadn't had a dream. When I said this, she nodded. "I would have thought it a dream or a hallucination myself except for one thing. From my vantage point I'd been able to see over the hedges and round the bend in the road, and I had noticed a blue car standing in the entrance to a field. It was still hidden from me when I recovered and continued my walk, but when I rounded the bend, there was the car and field entrance just as I had seen them. So I knew that for a few moments I had left my body and risen above it. I am sure that's what happened to you."

I think she convinced me because afterwards I tried again and again to repeat the experience but always failed. Perhaps a man only gets one chance and if he throws it away it is gone forever. What it all means, I cannot say. I can only ask the question.

Shortly after this experience, Shelagh and I had cause to celebrate. We found two rooms in a house at Greenpoint. The rent was £18 per month but although it was beyond our means, we hardly gave it thought at the time. We had to get away, if only for the sake of our future relations with the rest of the family.

To reach the house one had to walk from the bus route up a steep road which I believe was called Ravenscliff. It was a road I always associate with cricket. England were playing South Africa in Johannesburg at the time, and as I climbed the road from work one evening I could hear the cricket score emanating from radios and open windows. With Hutton and Washbrook batting, England were three hundred runs for no wickets. Far off days indeed!

The rest of my memories connected with that house are only fragmentary. I remember it had a fig tree in the garden and our rooms were full of old-fashioned furniture. I also remember Peter crying a great deal. Finding nothing wrong with him, our doctor told us it was just a baby doing what babies do, and if we picked him up and made a fuss of him, he would decide crying was a worthwhile pastime. So we were told to leave him be.

But such advice is difficult to follow when one has just moved in to someone else's home. After two nights of it, our nerves cracked and we ministered to him. After that he cried for most of the time we were there.

In making the move we had hoped to find some domestic peace at last and in one sense we had. But we soon became aware of the price we were paying for it. With £18 a month rent to pay and £1 10 month for my medical expenses, we had £7 a month to live on.

How Shelagh, bless her, managed I shall never know. Every penny had to be accounted for. During that summer I truly believe we were poorer in our living standards than any black servant in the city. Yet somehow we avoided taking more than a few pounds from our contingency fund.

A distant cousin of Mrs Mac, Kathleen Harte, came to our rescue as autumn arrived. She offered us her house at Mouille Point for £10 per month while she stayed up country with friends. We could have the house for sixteen weeks.

Because of its position in the bay, Mouille Point was notorious for its sea mists and a nearby lighthouse booming out its sepulchral warnings. These factors were nothing to us when we realised we would have another £8 a month to spend on food and clothing.

Without our knowing it, the move was also to have an huge influence on our future. After being there a week or two, Shelagh took Peter up country to visit some relations. She was away for three weeks and as we were now some distance from the friends I had made at Clifton, I found myself somewhat lost and restless in the evenings. So I bought an old, second-hand typewriter for a couple of pounds and began jotting down thoughts and ideas. I then tried a little poetry as I had done in my early wartime years.

Nothing more was needed. Suddenly my old craving to write was back. This was what I had always wanted to do. This was the world of creation where every dream could be fulfilled. This was the world where a man could become Pegasus (or even a dove) and fly on golden wings from the boredom of those four office walls.

I realised now the wish had always been there but the events of recent years had suffocated it. Now I knew it was something I must do and the discovery excited me.

I told it to Shelagh on her return and instead of laughing at my whim she encouraged me to pursue it. With this incentive I wrote my first short story. It was a sentimental piece called Pride, based on the wonderful bulldog I had known as a child and who had saved my life. I sent it to the Outspan, which at the time was South Africa's top-selling magazine, and when they bought it for £5 and a second story I wrote about a young fighter pilot, I nearly resigned my job. What was I doing in that unhappy office when I could make an enjoyable living writing short stories?

My absurd ambitions were brought to a shuddering halt when my third story was rejected. My fourth, fifth and sixth suffered the same fate. My euphoria nose-dived. Was I just a pipe dreamer after all and had my two stories been only flashes in the pan?

My saviour has always been the realist in me that walks alongside the romantic. I gave it careful thought and decided I had been expecting to enter a highly-competitive profession without serving my apprenticeship. By pure luck I'd had my first two efforts accepted but if I were to succeed I needed much more than luck.

As Shelagh had been as excited as I with my first two successes, we discussed the situation together. I told her I would like to devote five nights a week to learning my trade before I sent material out again. In that way I wouldn't flood the market with unsuitable material and I wouldn't risk being discouraged by rejections (although I never believed that I would be). The weekends we would keep free for tennis or other activities that we could afford.

Although this would mean many boring evenings for her, Shelagh told me to go ahead. So, from the next Monday, the routine began. I would arrive back home around 6pm when Shelagh would have dinner waiting for me. By six thirty I would be sitting down at the typewriter or studying fictional works by successful authors. Although ten thirty was supposed to close the night's work, I would sometimes continue to midnight and beyond. This was to be my routine for the next three years.

## SEVENTEEN

During this apprenticeship period I continued to write short stories because I soon realised that a writer must keep on writing scripts in order to learn from his mistakes. But I was now introducing into them the lessons I was learning and so they began to improve in plot construction and characterisation. Nevertheless, although I liked some of them, for a full year I resisted the temptation to submit them to magazines. By this time I was conscious how much better I could make them if I continued with my studies.

But life had to go on during this time and the problem of accommodation remained as difficult as ever. In what seemed no time at all our sixteen weeks were over and we were urgently seeking another place in which to live.

This time we were lucky. One of the Clifton tennis players, a middle-aged man named Dave Williams, had obtained a lease on a bungalow at Bakoven, and was planning to move into it with his girl friend, Sue. Bakoven was a village two miles past Clifton on the coast road that ran to Hout Bay. The bungalow itself was one of half a dozen built in a tiny bay below the road. Knowing our need, Dave offered to share it with us on a fifty-fifty basis. As the rent was £20 a month, this meant we would be paying no more than we were paying at Mouille Point.

The offer was only for six months. The land along that entire coast, including Clifton itself, belonged to the Admiralty and the Admiralty decreed that no bungalows or parts of bungalows sited there could be let for more than six months at one time. But to us six months was a reprieve and the offer delighted us.

It would have been hard to imagine a more idyllic setting. The bungalows were built at the foot of a cliff, with a tiny private beach before them. Huge granite rocks stood like sentinels on either side of the small bay and during the high spring tides the sea reached almost to the bungalow steps. Behind the bay and the coast road, the mountains seemed to soar almost perpendicularly into the sky.

If the days were radiant, moonlit evenings were almost unbelievably beautiful. The mountains would be dark and mysterious, the lapping waves would murmur music, and the sea would carry a silver pathway to the horizon. Even I, intoxicated by my new interest, would sometimes leave my typewriter and climb with Shelagh on one of the great rocks where we would sit and listen to the night.

From a domestic point of view, this was perhaps the happiest period we had known. Freed at last from strife and pressure, our only problems now were physical ones and so were bearable. Provided we could find ten pounds a month for rent, we could relax and enjoy our marriage and our child. Dave and Sue, much in love, were pleasant companions and shared the bungalow with equity and tolerance. Peter had recovered from his crying bouts and was now a normal and happy child. In all, it was a golden interlude and we made the most of every day, more so perhaps because we knew they had to end in a few months.

Bakoven did have its exciting moments, however. One evening, while we were listening to the radio, a member of the Fire Service interrupted the programme and asked for able-bodied men to help fight the fire that was raging on the mountain. Until then we had known nothing about it but on running outside we saw the sea was stained red to the horizon. Turning, we saw the mountain behind us was burning like a huge torch. With the south-east wind blowing, it was spreading rapidly downwards and towards the houses of Camps Bay.

As the calls for volunteers continued, I changed into old clothes and made my way to Camps Bay where fire fighting parties were being organised. I was given a beater's brush and sent with half a dozen other men to climb the mountain above the bay.

As we approached the fire, it sounded like approaching thunder. It was sweeping down the mountain on a wide front and clumps of pine trees, with their resin turned into gas by the heat, were exploding like shells. As we came nearer smoke bit into our eyes and the wind flung sparks forward like incandescent hail.

It was soon obvious to me that we had as much chance of stopping the inferno as a child's spade stopping the tide. In fact we could easily become a liability because not only was the fire, fanned by the wind, advancing faster than a man could run, but its flames were running along the dongas (ravines) that fissured the mountain. As they were full of dry vegetation, tongues of flame could sweep along them like water, and then leap up and encircle a party of beaters. As we were half-blinded by the smoke, the danger was real. I was told later that more than one man had died on the mountain in that way.

I would like to say I did a small part in checking that fire before it reached the houses but it would be a lie. After two or three hours of stumbling about half-blinded and beating out tiny fires caused by sparks, we were withdrawn. Even so, we stayed to watch the professional fire fighters at work and to see the fire checked before Camps Bay was destroyed.

For me, however, the night was not wasted. I made notes of the fire, which we were told later was one of the biggest in Cape Town's history and could be seen by ships a hundred miles away, and when I came to write my first novel, a fire was prominent in it.

We were playing a great deal of tennis at this time, a game we both loved. As our relations with Mrs Mac had improved almost as soon as we left her bungalow, she would sometimes look after Peter for us. Otherwise he would sit and play quite happily with his toys beneath the umpire's chair. He seemed to like watching us play, bringing humorous quips from players and spectators alike that one day he would become a tennis star.

It was while we were at Bakoven that we moved to a larger tennis club in Seapoint, called West Point. Shelagh was an excellent player and we felt she ought to be extended more. This soon paid off because within a month she was playing in the Grand Challenge League. I managed to get into one of the teams myself and the following year was made club captain. So in our free time we lived a pleasant enough life, although how we afforded it remains a mystery because my medical bills were never less than ten pounds a month. Moreover, because of the damage the amoeba had done to my intestines, I was forced to eat bland foods, which were more expensive than the normal variety. I suppose we managed because neither of us drank much or spent money on other pleasures.

Our six months passed quickly, as good things tend to do, and soon we were once again searching for accommodation. Hearing that two rooms were coming on the market on 4th Beach, we made urgent enquiries and found they were the lower part of a bungalow built halfway up the cliff. Although the rent was twelve pounds a month and the accommodation tiny compared with the Bakoven bungalow, we had no choice but to take it.

It was, in fact, a maid's quarters. With the bungalow built on stilts to keep it level, the two rooms had been created by boarding in the stilts. The job had been poorly done: a huge piece of granite rock protruded into the tiny kitchen and when our sofa bed was set down in the other room, we had to climb over it to reach Peter's cot. In front of these rooms was a stoep that overlooked the beach and the sea. A narrow flight of steps, running past the bungalow, linked the beaches to the road above.

In spite of it being a far cry from the Bakoven bungalow in terms of comfort, we were still on that beautiful coast and we found consolation in that. At the same time the site of the rooms on the cliff had its drawbacks. One Saturday night, after playing in a tennis match, I returned home to find Shelagh unusually agitated and cross with me for being so late back. Puzzled by behaviour that was totally unlike her, I told her we had won a match we had expected to lose and had enjoyed a few beers afterwards to celebrate. When she told me I ought to think more about my family, I knew something was wrong and put on my most conciliatory face. At that she threw herself into my arms, and then pointed to a corner of the tiny room.

Lying there were two halves of a scorpion that must have been eight inches long when in full health. Apparently it had crawled through the outer door and been making for Peter's cot when she had attacked it with a carving knife. Killing it had not been easy: it had wrapped itself round the knife and attempted to sting her. With Peter in mind, she had shaken it off and finally killed it, but afterwards, woman-like, had been unable to sweep out the remains.

Apart from tennis and my writing, our other relaxation at this time

*Shelagh and I on holiday in Cape Town - late 40's*

*Myself and Peter Clifton, 1949-50*

was poker. Here mention should be made about the cultural differences in South Africa to Britain. Here — certainly before the advent of television — evenings with friends would usually be spent in conversation as our days with Johnnie Gemmel had been spent. In South Africa conversation was at a premium. One did things instead, like playing cards, playing tennis, or going for a swim. It was the evenings in conversation that Shelagh loved and one of the reasons she loved life in Britain.

*Shelagh and I with tennis trophy, circa 1950*

But we were in South Africa now and so when our Clifton tennis friends visited us we played poker with the little kitchen the venue. Because of my writing schedule, these games were on Saturday evenings. We would put Peter to sleep and then the game would begin.

It would be hard to imagine anything more Bohemian, with the huge rock making a table for coffee cups or wine and the outer door opening to a view of the white beaches and the breaking waves.

At the same time it is something of a mystery how we could afford to play cards at that time. But play we did, and if we lost we just pulled our belts a little tighter. Yet in truth we seldom did lose. Shelagh had been introduced to the game by her brother and his friends when she was young, and so was not only an excellent player but had become accustomed to playing with men. I had learned the game in many a hard school during the war and so it seldom happened that we both lost on the same night. More often than not we won a few shillings which went towards our housekeeping costs.

So it was a Bohemian life we lived during our six months on the cliff side and although it had its drawbacks it has left me with many happy memories.

# EIGHTEEN

It was during our tenure in that bungalow that the Nationalist Government of South Africa introduced its infamous apartheid laws into the Constitution. Soon the newspapers and radio were full of little else as one draconian law followed another.

It would be untrue to say that our domestic situation was affected to any extent. Our contact with the black and coloured population was limited to Maggie in Mrs McGrath's bungalow and an odd coloured workman called in to do maintenance or repairs. They made no comment on apartheid, no doubt expecting all Europeans to be unsympathetic, and so we remained relatively ignorant of their problems.

The same was true of the majority of Europeans, certainly those in Cape Town. We had little if any idea of the distress the laws were inflicting on the coloured races, and like human beings everywhere, because we didn't see the miseries we tended to ignore them or assume they were exaggerated.

To my personal shame it was some months before I began to see the falsehoods behind the Government's claims that the laws were of benefit to all. My first revelation came one morning while at work. Around 10 a.m. we heard the howl of a police car and gazing from our office windows saw four armed policemen run into the factory. Five minutes later they came out with the foreman, an Indian called Naidoo, bundled him into the car, and drove away.

We couldn't understand it. Naidoo was efficient, trustworthy, and respected by everyone from the management to the factory workers whom he supervised. Indeed, his very status as foreman was proof of the high regard in which he was held, for, although it was true the firm was foreign owned and therefore not so rigid in its interpretation of the colour bar, it was nevertheless most unusual for any firm based in South Africa to employ a coloured worker in any position of responsibility. Yet Naidoo had held the position with great success for a number of years. During that time he had married a local coloured girl and had a family of two children.

As the police gave no reason for this sudden arrest, the directors made enquiries why their foreman had been taken away so arbitrarily. They received a tart explanation. Records showed that fifteen years earlier Naidoo had left Natal without a pass. It had always been against the law for Indians to do this, but under Smith's government the laws had not been rigidly enforced. Under apartheid such laxity would no longer be tolerated. Naidoo would pay the price for his transgression.

Naidoo did pay. Two weeks later we heard he had received five years hard labour. Our directors made a protest but they might as well have tried to stem the incoming sea. Without even being allowed to see and say goodbye to his frantic wife, Naidoo was sent back to Natal with other 'criminals' to serve his punishment. None of us ever saw him again.

My second insight into the brutality of the new laws came from two old people who lived in a tiny apartment behind Boy's workshop. I had often seen them when I worked with him. Supporting one another, the man wearing an old sun hat that hid his face and the woman a kind of veil, they would occasionally emerge from the lane and pass by the shop window as they did their shopping. They looked so very old and vulnerable, so timid of people who passed them by, that I had occasionally felt curiosity but never thought to ask Boy if he knew anything about them.

They were brought vividly back to my mind one evening when Boy called round to see us. When I asked him if the new laws were causing him any new problems, he shook his head. "Not as long as we don't let blacks do any skilled or semi-skilled work. They're even stricter about that than the old Government was. But plenty of people are being affected. Like those two old folk who live behind the workshop."

I stirred at this. "Who are that couple? I often thought of asking you."

"They're not married," he told me. "They're just living together. They've gotten away with it so far but you can see they're scared stiff now. He only takes her out when it's dusk and they don't go shopping together any more."

I was intrigued. "But why? What are they so afraid of?"

It was then I heard a story that I found profoundly moving. It seemed the old man had been a free-lance diamond prospector in German West Africa before World War One and had gone down with cholera in a particularly lonely diggings. Near to death, he had been found by a coloured girl, who after weeks of hardship had nursed him back to health.

It was now the character of the man had showed itself. In the colour-bar context of the time, ninety-nine per cent of Europeans would have given the girl a few pounds and sent her on her way. But it seemed this man had understood the working of the human heart. He had known that one often grows to love the things one works and suffers for, and after suffering and caring for him, the girl had fallen deeply in love.

So he had not sent her away. He did not marry her. Perhaps that was asking too much for a man of his time, or perhaps he could not find anyone to marry them. Whatever the reason, he had pretended she was his wife wherever he went, and only those who have lived among racists can imagine the heartbreaks and problems the couple must have suffered during the next forty odd years in lost jobs, humiliation, spite and cruelty, the list is endless. But they had remained steadfast right up to old age, which they must have hoped would give them security.

But not any longer. Under the new Miscegenation Act that forbade white and coloureds to have intimate relationships, they were breaking the law by living together. Every time they ventured from their home, a passer-by might report them to the police. Whether the law would be enforced was neither here nor there. After half a century of loyalty, they had the fear of being torn apart and punished. Apartheid was making their lives a living hell.

Nothing I heard or saw affected me more deeply than that true story. No honeyed words of politicians, no arguments that all races would be better off if they were segregated, could counter the human tragedy of those two old people. If laws punish people for their loyalty and their love, then those laws were evil. From that moment on I was an enemy of apartheid.

Our six months in the bungalow ran out that year but this time we had no need to search the newspapers and comb the streets for rooms. The bungalow next to Tandragee, Mrs Mac's home, had come up for sale and with her menopausal problems over and her true character restored, she decided to buy it as an investment and let us be its tenants. However, because the Admiralty laws forbade the occupier of one bungalow to own another, the new bungalow had to be put under my name on the understanding it would revert to Mrs Mac or Monica if ever we moved away.

When this small deception finally went through, our relief was immense. If we were prepared to stay there, our roaming days were over.

It was a charming little bungalow with a small back garden overlooking the rocks and sea coves that stretched between Clifton and Camps Bay. Our monthly rent was only nine pounds, and as the bungalow had three bedrooms and we needed only two, we let the front one to a young Austrian for ten shillings a week. This meant we would have another two pounds a month for ourselves. We felt we had won the local sweepstake!

With our accommodation problem solved at last, I wondered if I should write my parents and broach again the subject of their emigration. They had not mentioned it for over a year, which made us think they didn't really want to make the move. For my part, having become aware of the injustices of apartheid, I was now uneasy what the future might bring. So I decided to procrastinate and no mention was made of emigration in our current letters.

It was at this time that I heard about my grandmother's death, just after her ninety-second birthday. Almost to my surprise, the news saddened me. It was true she had inflicted cruel wounds on my family and, as I was to discover later, some of the scars were only paper-thin. But she had been a part of my young life and I had long ago come to terms with her behaviour. So I regretted her death and my inability to attend her funeral. Not long afterwards I wrote a short story incorporating my feelings which I called Candle in the Veld.

Winter passed and the white beaches of Clifton began to fill again with swimmers and sun-worshippers. The beauty of the place, with its granite rocks, its blue sea, and its towering mountains was a temptation on my return home from work, and occasionally I would steal an hour or two off my schedule to play on the beach with Peter, who was now a sturdy, good-looking child blessed (or cursed) with a sensitive nature. But on the whole I kept to my working schedule and reserved the weekends for tennis, swimming, and outings.

By this time I had fifteen short stories written and felt I had learned enough to try them on the big world. But the big world in literary terms were the British and USA markets, and they were thousands of miles away.

This distance was a chain on my ambitions. With air mail prohibitively expensive, every story had to be sent by sea mail. This meant a too-and-fro journey of at least six weeks, and only those stricken by the writing bug know how long such weeks can be. At times they seemed endless, particularly when a magazine kept a story for months before rejecting it, as magazines are prone to do.

Nevertheless, although months of frustration followed, I did have one success that year. An English magazine bought a short story called Twelve Peaks to the Sky, which I based on a tribal superstition. I only received £10 for it but my delight and relief couldn't have been greater had I won a literary prize. The long drought had ended at last and I had broken into the British market! After dozens of disappointments, I felt the self-denial of my apprenticeship was justified.

I was further encouraged when a new monthly magazine named The London Mystery Magazine, began taking my stories. Again I only received £10 a story and that with the agreement that I surrendered the copyright of the story after accepting the cheque. Too naive or too glad to have the acceptance, I was not to know what this loss of copyright would mean in the years ahead. Instead, as I sold a further half dozen stories to the magazine, I began to believe the unbelievable. That perhaps one day I might become a professional author.

It was this ambition that gave me the desire to write a novel.

Surely a man couldn't call himself a writer until he had at least one novel under his belt, I thought. But what would its theme be? I searched newspapers but could find nothing that stirred me. Then one day I heard Russell talking to Mrs Nolan about the new laws and I could have shouted aloud at my discovery. The theme had been right under my nose all this time. I would write a novel about apartheid.

Full of excitement I went home that evening and discussed the idea with Shelagh. Finding apartheid as unfair and despicable as I did, she thought it an excellent idea but felt we should give it careful thought before developing a plot worthy of the theme.

I shared her feelings. It would have been relatively easy to construct a story in which all Nationalists were bullies who kept the blacks subjugated at all costs, but we knew this was not always true. One of the members of our tennis club, an Afrikaner named Johann Mostert, was a doctor in the Groote Schuur Hospital, and although in principle he supported the apartheid movement, no one could have shown more charity to the black and coloured communities than he. From October onwards he would begin collecting money and toys from his friends, colleagues, and acquaintances, and with their help he would throw a Christmas party for over a hundred children in District Six.

Critics would call it patronage, paternalism, or even a sop to guilt, but I knew the man better than that. He genuinely believed the races did not mix well and would fare better apart, but that did not diminish a sympathy for the downtrodden and the sick. He also loved children whatever their colour.

Another highly-educated young Afrikaner we knew, Aubrey Haupt, was the son of a millionaire farmer in the Orange Free State. The father, a fanatical Nationalist, warned Aubrey that if he ever fell into the liberal and decadent ways of the Cape, he would be instantly disinherited. Yet we who played tennis with Aubrey knew he was giving two night classes a week to black students, a crime that would have given his father apoplexy had it reached his ears.

With friends of this kind, I knew my novel could be no black and white tract. For that matter, who was I to pontificate? When had I spent months of my free time to give coloured children their greatest day of the year or sacrificed my evenings for black education? A novel that did not tell the truth did not seem to either of us worth writing.

And yet whatever characters I used, I knew the book must in the final analysis condemn apartheid as a cruel political system. The more I thought about a plot, the greater the problems seemed to grow. Within my set target, how was I going to show a fair picture of South Africa, of the disparate views of its peoples and its races, of the British, the Afrikaners, the Malays, the Indians, the Coloureds, the Blacks? And if, as I must, come down against apartheid, what solution was I going to put into its place? For it had always seemed to me that a man should offer an answer to a problem before he attacks it.

I was, of course, being absurdly ambitious. I ought to have settled on a simple tale of one coloured person's experiences as apartheid destroyed his life. But I was young and full of the desire to be fair to all. I had a wonderful theme and I wanted to explore every intriguing facet of it.

What I could not know at the time was that I was embarking on the most difficult form of fiction. My intentions were to weave a fictional story into the cruel facts and consequences of the apartheid laws. With no writers or editors to advise me, I had no way of knowing that this type of novel is the most difficult of all to write. No novel is easy but at least in pure fiction the imponderables are flexible and can be adjusted to fit the time scale of a story. But a novel based on facts and dates allows no such freedom.

An analogy is a creeper growing up a wall. Initially it is free to grow in whatever direction it chooses. But when a lattice is erected above it, its creepers are now limited in the direction they can take.

Such is the problem of a novel written around facts. With its plot construction so limited it can cause problems on almost every page.

Happy in my ignorance, I plunged into research with enthusiasm. In one way I was well placed to do this. By this time Shelagh and I were playing Grand Challenge tennis and were often invited to tournaments held up and down the country. As sometimes these tournaments were held by rich Afrikaner farmers, if one kept one's eyes and ears open, much could be learned about apartheid and how it was being received in rural communities.

An example of this came that very year. Shelagh and I were invited to a day tournament near Stellenbosch and after the mornings play we and all the other competitors were invited to have lunch with a local Afrikaner farmer.

Like so many of his kind, he was rich and his table showed it. It groaned under huge sides of beef, bowls of fruit, and bottles of wine and spirits. Shelagh and I were seated in the centre of the long table. Opposite us were the farmer's three sons, ranging from around eighteen to twenty six. The farmer himself, a patriarchal figure with a long salt-and-pepper beard, sat at the head of the table. Although much of the conversation was in Afrikaans, which I could not speak, Shelagh told me later it had been mostly about farming and tennis.

But its innocence ceased when coffee and liqueurs were being served. Suddenly the youngest of the three sons, a lad with a shock of blond hair, addressed me across the table in English. "I've heard you are writing a book about South Africa, meneer. Is it true?"

To this day I have no idea how he had heard, because for obvious reasons both Shelagh and I had kept quiet about the novel's purpose. Conscious the question could open delicate doors, I tried an evasive answer. "I do scribble a little, yes. It's a hobby of mine."

"I think you do more than scribble, meneer. What is this book about?"

Beneath the table I felt Shelagh's leg nudge mine. I took the hint "My impressions of South Africa, I suppose."

"Do those impressions include apartheid?"

Suddenly all the conversation around us ceased. Aware of it, I chose my words carefully. "I suppose it might come into it somewhere. But it's early days yet."

"Can I ask what your views are, meneer?"

Shelagh nudged me again. "I don't think this is the time to discuss politics, do you?" I said. "Let's talk about something else, shall we?"

"But I want to talk about politics, meneer. I understand you don't like apartheid. And I wonder what right you English have to come over here and write about things that don't concern you."

I am afraid that was it for me. My Mr Hyde, already bristling under the attack of this young character, brushed aside my caution and answered in kind. "I think they should concern everyone who believes in justice and fair play. Don't you think so?"

"That's rubbish and nonsense. They only concern us who have lived here for hundreds of years. What right do you think you have to come over here and tell us how to live?"

I don't remember how Mr Hyde answered that but it must have been to the point. Although the youngster's brothers tried to grab hold of him, he leapt to his feet and began shouting at me in Afrikaans.

His insults meant nothing to me, who could not speak the language, but I was conscious of the distress they were causing Shelagh. So I pushed Mr Hyde back into his cave and tried to calm the youngster down. But before I could get half a dozen words out there was a thump and a roar that made every glass on the table tremble. "Skaam jou! How dare you insult my guest this way? Vra dadelik om verskoning!"

I couldn't believe what I was seeing. There was the old man, who must have privately agreed with every word his son had said, on his feet and thundering with rage. As he thrust out an arm as thick as a cudgel at the startled boy, I thought of Moses descending from Sinai and catching the Israelites having their orgy. "You will apologize to my guest!" he roared. "You will apologize or you will leave this house and never return! Do you hear me?"

There was no doubt he meant every word of it. I tried to mediate. "It's all right, sir. He's only young and hot-headed. And in any case I didn't know what he was saying."

He brushed my mediation aside as if it were an irritating fly. "He will apologize to you or he will never live in this house again.

Never! Do you hear me, skaam jou?"

To cut the story short I received my apology and we went back to tennis. But I had learned that day there were some Nationalists who still put hospitality before politics. As men with such priorities are hard to dislike, I knew it was not going to make my novel any easier to write.

## NINETEEN

Towards the end of 1951 I decided I needed to explore District Six. It took little imagination to guess that a violent regime like apartheid was certain to inflame those blacks and coloureds who had always resented the colour bar and some might already be inciting an equally violent resistance. If so, District Six was a likely place to ferment it. But how could I, an Englishman who could not speak Afrikaans, do research in there to find out?

A young coloured man at my place of work called Michael Tybeck came to my rescue. He knew of my dislike of apartheid and when he found out I wanted to go around the shabeens (drinking houses) of District Six, he offered to take me himself.

I should never have allowed him to take the risk because if my disguise and intention became known, he would probably be in greater danger than myself. But by this time the novel was controlling me and I accepted his offer.

So a few evenings later we met in readiness for our venture. Michael was dressed like a man about town in a gaudy jacket and slacks, and I, looking like a labourer, wearing dark glasses and a pair of dirty overalls.

District Six, (which has since been razed to the ground), was a forbidding place. Once it had been a residential area but that had been in the early days of Cape Town. Now it was a festering slum of decaying houses and small dirty shops. The air was hot and fetid and popular music blared out from open windows. Barefooted children played street games, flies crawled over fruit stalls, mangy dogs pawed at the litter that clogged the alleyways, and shabbily dressed men hung in groups around street corners. The ambience was despair and I couldn't help thinking what a tinderbox it was for agitators. Michael must have read my thoughts. "If you think this is bad you ought to go and see Windermere. People live in dug-outs or cardboard boxes out there."

He checked me at the entrance of an alleyway. Down it three men were separating pieces of offal that lay on sheets of soggy newspaper. Behind them a queue of black women waited. Finishing his task, a man waved the first woman forward. She was young with a black shawl wrapped around her head. Tied to her back with another shawl was a baby. She pointed enquiringly at a piece of offal. When the man quoted a price, she shook her head and pointed to a second piece. Again the price was too high. Finally the man impatiently thrust a length of intestine at her and took the few coppers from her hand. As she moved away, a second black woman moved forward.

"It's called the offal market," Michael told me. "They have bigger ones in Windermere and the other black townships. It's the blacks who're usually the customers: they're the ones at the bottom of the ladder. Everyone exploits them."

We visited two shabeens that day, keeping to our pre-arranged plan in which I slumped down on a bench pretending I was too drunk to talk and Michael bought the drinks. This way I could see everything that happened around me.

There seemed no shortage of liquor. Although the law had always forbidden liquor for the blacks, raw brandy seemed plentiful. Rumour had it that the large distilleries made a profitable sideline by allowing inferior brandy to seep into the coloured market and the authorities turned a blind eye to it. From the quantities we saw that week, I am certain it was true. Gin palaces had helped the Victorians to keep their poor subservient, so one could well believe the same practice applied here.

At first I was disappointed with the shabeens. Drunks were plentiful, men squabbled with one another or exchanged agga (marijuana) cigarettes, but I could relate nothing to apartheid.

Our fourth visit changed all that. We made this visit at night and found a large drinking hall with the most villainous character I'd ever seen guarding its entrance, a coloured man with eyes as beady as a snake and a long knife scar down one cheek. At first he didn't want to let us enter, but after Michael slipped him a few shillings he stood aside and let us through.

We found ourselves in the largest beer hall we had yet seen. There was also the largest crowd we had seen. Men and women were six deep round the walls and their excitement and prurient expressions suggested the entertainment was anything but music hall fare. Lights blazed down on the centre of the hall where a large rug was resting.

The air stank of marijuana which both men and women were smoking. Trying not to draw attention to myself by coughing, I followed Michael to a site where we tried to be as inconspicuous as possible.

It was not long before the hum of excitement turned into one of anticipation. Men surged forward and women cackled as a huge naked black man emerged from a doorway dragging a screaming, partly-dressed woman after him. At first I thought she was white but as he dragged her beneath the lights and threw her down on to the rug I saw she was a black or coloured woman disguised with some white dye.

The excitement of the crowd was now turning to fever heat. Men and women shouted encouragement and jibes as the woman cowered on the rug while the black stood astride her. Turning, he shouted something to the crowd and they roared encouragement back at him. Then he leaned down and ripped the clothes from the woman.

The scene became a surrealist nightmare. Drugged eyes glowed with lust as the black figure tore the woman's legs apart and poised over her. Then, as she screamed, he threw himself forward, pinned down her arms, and began raping her. As her screams filled the hall, men and women around us began to fornicate.

Although I knew the raped woman was only play acting, I felt deadly sick and wanted to leave. As I motioned to Michael, he nodded and we edged our way through the crowd to the door. We reached it and were just about to slip outside when the villainous character we had met earlier grabbed Michael's arm and challenged him. Michael said something back but the man kept his grip and shouted for help.

Michael shoved him away and turned to me. "He's guessed. Run!"

How we escaped I shall never know although I believe my unarmed combat training was of some help. We dashed down alleyways, tripped over piles of garbage, leapt over walls, and all the time heard urgent yells and shouts behind us as half a dozen skollies armed with clubs and knives gave chase.

If Michael had not known the way out, we would never have made it. As it was, panting, bruised, and desperate, we managed to reach one of the wider roads that ran through the district and from it reached the main thoroughfare that led into the city. There we were safe.

We never went again. We knew the alarm would have gone out and we would never escape a second time. But that night confirmed my belief. Repressive legislation will always have its reaction and militants will profit by inflaming the public to join their ranks. It is a thing all governments should remember.

But at the same time I should add that the experience in no way made me feel it justified apartheid's arguments and cruelties. The vast majority of its victims suffered its injustices with surprising patience and tolerance, and, as time was one day to show, with a forgiveness that astonished the world.

I finished the first draft of the novel early in 1952. It was huge, over 180,000 words. I called it *Laws be their Enemy* from Burke's famous speech back on the 8th October 1777. Never in my life had I worked so hard on anything. One chapter alone, my effort to suggest an alternative policy to apartheid in the climate of the time, was written twenty-five times before I had allowed it to go through.

As I had also added another twenty short stories to my collection and all the work had been done in the evenings and weekends, it is hard to know where I had found my energy from, particularly because I had not been in the best of health during those years.

Yet ironically this ill health had been an important factor in my construction of the novel. Realizing that if I made the story a black and white condemnation of apartheid few Afrikaners would read it, I had wanted its early chapters to deceive the book's intention and had needed the right character and construction to serve this purpose. My ill health had come to my aid here in the oddest way. Before my amoebic dysentery had been correctly diagnosed, my doctor had fed me with every drug listed in his medical library and any new ones that came on the market. The outcome had been a series of boils on my legs that rapidly turned into ulcers. They would start as a sharp needle prick, always on a vein or artery. By the next morning a large blister would form and quickly burst. It left beneath it an ugly sore with a hard centre that rapidly developed into a boil or ulcer.

I'd had these abscesses right through 1951. Although they were painful in the mornings when a standing position would increase the blood pressure in the legs, I hadn't paid them too much attention, perhaps because I was only getting one at a time, and because my faith in doctors had taken too many blows. Indeed, I had continued playing tennis throughout the year.

Nevertheless, by 1952 it was clear something was seriously wrong. I was now getting half a dozen ulcers at a time and they were spreading up my legs. As I wondered what action I should take, Johann Mostert came to my rescue. A regular visitor to our bungalow, he was very fond of Peter to whom he often used to bring little presents. Because of our friendship I had never thought to ask his advice on health problems, but one summer night when I was wearing shorts, he asked me about the plasters on my legs. When I told him their history, he asked if he might remove one of the plasters. On doing so, he showed immediate concern. "You can't leave this any longer, man. It could be serious. Let me have a blood specimen and I'll have it checked in our paths lab."

He wouldn't take no for an answer and went off with a sample of my blood. In a couple of days he came to see me. "It's what I thought. You've got a blood problem, almost certainly caused by all those drugs you've been given. It has to be treated or the ulcers will spread all over your body."

"So what do I do?" I asked. "Take more drugs?"

"You need one of the new strains of penicillin. It's called aureomycin. You need at least eight tablets a day. But I have to warn you they're expensive."

That was the last thing I wanted to hear. "How expensive?"

He grimaced. "Sixteen shillings a capsule. The stuff's new and hard to get."

I did a quick calculation. "That would be over six pounds a day. How long would I have to take them?"

"It's difficult to say. Perhaps three weeks to a month."

After the sacrifices Shelagh had made to keep our contingency fund more or less intact, I wasn't going to waste it on a few boils. "Then it's out of the question. Don't worry about it. It'll probably clear up on its own one of these days."

He said no more but after he had gone Shelagh took me to task. "That's what the fund is for. An emergency."

"But this isn't an emergency."

"Yes it is. I could tell from Johann's expression that it's serious."

I remained stubborn and we almost had a quarrel. But the next evening Johann arrived with a large bottle of capsules. "Two after every meal and two before you go to bed," he told me. "They ought to do the trick."

"I'm not paying that sort of money for them, Johann. It's bloody ridiculous."

He winked at the relieved Shelagh. "You don't have to, man. Take them as a gift from South Africa."

Realizing they were from the hospital, I argued no further and began taking them. The effect was magical. The blisters still formed for the next few days but after they burst there were no ulcers beneath them. After two weeks even the blisters went and I was cured.

I learned much later that the blood disease might have killed me if left unchecked. I also learned, to my shame, that Johann had paid for the capsules himself. But at the time one thought dominated all others. I had my major character for my novel. If I used a character like Johann, a believer in apartheid but a man of great kindness, at the beginning of my novel, it would give a reader no warning of what was to come later when through the story line my character discovers the inherent cruelty of the regime.

This is what I did and I owe the novel's success to Johann and his friendship. Many years later when I returned to South Africa, he was one of the first people I tried to contact. To my horror I learned he had committed suicide. It seemed he had been a homosexual and because homosexuality was a crime in the Union, he must have found the pressures too great to bear. Whenever I meet intolerance, I think of Johann and wonder if people will ever take note of the Christian message that God's house has many mansions and it is often only luck or our genes that decide which one is ours.

# TWENTY

It was around March 1952 that a restlessness borne of my writing began to affect me. My ambition to be a full-time writer was growing by the day and I was finding the waiting for mail from England more and more frustrating, particularly when my novel was near completion.

But at first I got no further than thinking about a return. After all our struggles, we had a home at last and a home in one of the most beautiful places in the world. To contemplate giving it up and returning to the kind of life we had known in England seemed folly of the worst kind. I would look at Shelagh and Peter, both healthy, sun-tanned and happy, and the very thought of tearing them away from that beautiful beach with its golden haze, its white waves, and glorious mountains seemed like sacrilege. How could I think of doing it to them? How could I think of doing it to myself?

The truth was I loved Clifton and knew there would never be a place I would love more. Then wouldn't it be madness to give it away for a pipe dream? More than likely my writing ambitions would fail and I would find myself back in another dreary office with no beautiful Clifton as a consolation.

Against this was my work in Woodstock, which I disliked more each passing day. There was also apartheid. Having had my eyes opened to its injustices, I didn't want Peter to grow up beneath it. With Shelagh liking apartheid no more than I, we would sometimes try to convince ourselves that we could insulate him from the political influences he would meet at school, but I doubted if either of us believed it. Hadn't some Germans tried to fight Nazism the same way, only to find their childrens' minds stolen for ever?

But there were three years before Peter would be at risk because in South Africa children didn't begin school until they were seven. That gave us over three years to procrastinate. Three years and perhaps even longer to enjoy the home we had once thought would never be ours.

So my thoughts swung like a pendulum that year. Yet with each passing week, the arguments to return to England grew stronger.

Why should I fail? By this time I'd had ten short stories published and those had been written in my spare time and suffered the handicap of distance. Surely if I lived in England and wrote full time I could produce and sell four times as many. I had not yet learned that Sod's Law does not operate that way.

On top of that there was the novel. I believed in it. But because of its content it would be impossible to market it in South Africa. Nor did the problems end there. The Nationalists were highly sensitive about their apartheid laws and there were already reports of prosecutions of its critics. As I was now a dual national with South African citizenship, I might be considered an enemy of the State if I managed to have it published overseas. This was one reason I hadn't already sent it away. With rumours circulating that mail was now being censored, I didn't want Shelagh involved in any legal action that might result.

To make matters worse I had again been in trouble with the police. On leaving work one evening, I had found myself waiting at the bus stop with an elderly coloured woman. When the bus arrived, I had stood aside for her to climb aboard. Seemingly irritated by my gesture, the conductor had rung his bell before the woman was safely on the platform and if I hadn't been there to catch her she would have had a nasty fall. Angered, I had run after the bus, jumped aboard, and told the conductor what I thought of him. In turn he had stopped the bus and called on the driver for help. Within minutes the police had arrived and I was in danger of being arrested for attacking the conductor.

To be fair to South Africans, it was not a typical scenario. Bus conductors in the Union were not drawn from the top ranks of society, and perhaps the fact that many of them had coloured blood themselves while being classed as Europeans made them defend their classification more aggressively than others of the same racial group. But it did nothing to improve my views of apartheid, while at the same time making me aware my name was already down in some police file. This would hardly further my case if my novel was considered subversive.

These were some of the conflicting thoughts that plagued me as the year wore on. I tried to suppress them but every time I looked at that huge novel into which I had poured in so much time and energy, the greater the yearning grew until at last I was forced to discuss the entire thing with Shelagh.

As I expected, wonderful girl that she was, she was prepared to return with me to England if that was what I wanted. But as she spoke, I imagined her giving a little inner sigh. This, after all, was her country and I was asking her to leave it again and to give up everything we had struggled for during the last six years. All for a personal and improbable dream. I had never appreciated her love and loyalty more and did try to be patient, but she had not forgotten because a couple of weeks later she brought up the question of our finances if we did return. During our recent life in the bungalow, because of our reduced costs and my short story sales, we had boosted our contingency fund back to a little over five hundred pounds. If we laid aside our return fare, we could go back to England where, if we lived on the tightest possible budget, our money could last for two years. If in that time my writing efforts failed, we could still return to South Africa and to the bungalow which \Mrs Mac promised to keep for us.

At the time it seemed an excellent compromise. If I failed, we would be no worse off in South Africa than when we had arrived five years earlier. In fact, we would be far better off because I would still have made some literary contacts in England during our two years there and still have a South African home to return to.

I knew it had all been thought out for my benefit and I loved Shelagh for it. At the same time I knew its risks and the sacrifice it would be for her. Nevertheless the very next day I went in to see the firm's Managing Director, a tall, white-haired Englishman named Armitage. He looked surprised when I entered his office. "Hello, Smith. How did you know I wanted to see you this morning?"

My mind was too occupied to take much notice of his remark. "I didn't know," I said. "I came to . . . ."

He cut my explanation off short. "Never mind. You're here now. I wanted to talk to you about this new factory we've been building in Port Elizabeth. As you know, it's finished now and we're looking for staff. I've discussed it with my fellow directors and we've decided to put you in charge of the main office. Of course it will mean an increase in salary."

I couldn't believe what I was hearing. "What kind of increase, sir?"

"You'll start on seventy pounds a month. Twice your present salary, I believe."

I felt he had leaned across his desk and hit me with a truncheon. He saw my expression and misunderstood. "What's the matter? Don't you fancy the move?"

It took me a full ten seconds to reply. "No. It isn't that. I came in this morning to resign."

He gave a start. "Resign? For heaven's sake, why?"

I told him. He stared at me as if I were mad. "You are going back to England to write stories? What sort of stories?"

"Short stories. Novels. Plays. I don't really know at the moment."

"But that's a hobby, not a job. You can't bring up a family on stories. What on earth put that idea into your head?"

How do you explain the passions and yearnings of a writer to a hard-headed business man? I knew no way. "I enjoy writing," I said weakly.

His laugh seemed as much to reassure himself he hadn't chosen an idiot for his new office than to make me see sense. "Well, we all have our hobbies, haven't we? But you won't want to resign now, will you? Not on twice your salary."

I was in free fall at that moment. I had fought down my doubts and misgivings all night and come to work with my courage screwed up to breaking point. And now he was doing this to me. If he were the devil himself, I thought, he could not be offering me greater temptation. I thought of Shelagh, how she had struggled on a pittance all these years and the little luxuries this salary would allow her, and there seemed no way I could be so selfish to follow my star when she might be the loser.

Time seemed to stop. Then I heard someone swallow and a hoarse voice that wasn't mine say the fateful words. "No, sir. I must do it. But I'm grateful for your offer."

He stared at me, then sank back into his chair as if glad that such an idiot would no longer be on his payroll. "You're mad," he muttered. "Quite mad."

I felt he must be right when I walked out of that office. I had been given a totally unexpected chance of saving my family from a wild gamble and I had turned it down. I walked out into the sunlight with my conscience flailing me at every step.

We sailed two weeks later. Friends and relations came to the quayside to see us off. As the ship sailed out into the bay and that lovely green Table Mountain began to sink on the horizon, I couldn't stifle the thought that there was no turning back now. We had burned all our bridges and I wondered if I would ever be able to forgive myself if the gamble failed.

# TWENTY-ONE

We docked at Southampton and took the train straight to Hull. My father met us at Paragon Station and I remember thinking he had aged during our absence, although the impression soon disappeared when he welcomed and embraced us.

It was Peter's first meeting with his grandfather and he looked startled when he was picked up and kissed. He had always been a shy child, so much so that during a ship's party for children, he had been too timid to collect his prize, and his eyes were wide with the mystery of it all when we took a taxi to my parents' home.

They were still living on Spring Bank West, the house they had taken to aid our escape from Sharpe. It had no garden and I remember my pang of guilt on realizing that because of that gesture my father had been denied his beloved hobby all these years. Because a young family had moved into the house, he and mother were now living in our old quarters on the top floor. We were given their front bedroom and our two trunks were stored in a box room.

It was a happy reunion with both parents seeing Peter for the first time. My mother thought he was the most beautiful child she had ever seen and could not take her eyes off him while we all caught up with our news. We learned that my father was still working for the sweet manufacturer and my mother was employed as the manageress of a confectionery shop. We also learned that in her Will my grandmother had left the two small houses she owned to my mother's sister, Lena. It seemed that even in death she had never forgiven mother for remaining loyal to my father. To her great credit, however, Lena had been unable to accept a bequest she felt belonged to my mother, and so had given her one of these houses. It was sited at the end of Northfield Road in West Hull.

But there was a problem. The house, still under a small mortgage, had a tenant, a widow. With my parents already having accommodation, they could not enforce an exchange under the present Housing Emergency Laws. With our arrival, however, the equation changed and they now felt they stood a reasonable chance of obtaining the house. Although at this point they had made no complaints, it wasn't long before the sound of squabbling voices below told Shelagh and I what they had put up with during the last five years. Aware we had been the cause, I decided to do all I could to help them obtain the bequested house.

Although conscious of our limited resources and of my need to begin work, Shelagh and I felt the reunion justified one celebration. So we hired a small car and the five of us spent three days together in the Lake District. The last two days were spent driving around the local countryside. Needless to say, Ruston Parva was high on our list, although the visit was saddened by the absence of Hannah who had died during our absence. Johnnie Gemmell, with whom we made joyful reunion the day after our arrival, accompanied us on these last two days.

With the short holiday over, I wasted no time beginning work. I had brought forty unpublished short stories over with me, and with the guidance of a writers' handbook, Shelagh and I began sending them out to magazines. At the same time I polished up my apartheid novel and sent it off to a book publisher. Full of hope, I then began my second novel.

This was based on a cutting I had seen in a South African newspaper just before we left. It was about a famous scientist who, suffering from acute depression, had been given a pre-frontal lobotomy operation. The article had gone on to suggest that while the operation could cure depression and some other neuroses, it had the unfortunate effect of destroying a man's creative ability.

I had latched on this as a dramatic theme for a novel. Supposing I turned the scientist into a famous musical composer. If I made him too depressed to make the decision himself and he had a wife who loved his work and knew he would never have chosen such a loss himself, would not the possibilities make it a powerful and different kind of work? The idea had excited me and I had decided to make it my second novel.

But although every day counted if we were to succeed before our money ran out, the hard facts of life could not be ignored. My parents' flat was only meant to accommodate two people and our arrival was putting unfair pressure on them. Told by a solicitor that it might be months before we could petition for my mother's house, I went to the local Housing Department to ask if an exchange could be arranged.

To my surprise we were offered a three-bed-roomed council house within a fortnight. The exact address I forget but it was in north east Hull, one of four houses built around a cul- de-sac. Using my father's van we moved into it at our first opportunity and so found more room to spread ourselves and for me to start work.

And work I did. I began writing around 8.30 am, took fifteen minutes off for lunch, the same for dinner, and worked on until 8 or 9 p.m. Not five days a week but seven. And sometimes I found the energy to work during the nights too. Perhaps Yoga, which I had continued to practise since my mystical experience at Clifton, helped me to concentrate for periods of seven to eight hours at a stretch.

There was no other way. With my eyes on our small bank balance, I knew I must push myself to the limit, not just by producing another novel but also by writing other forms of drama, because at this time I had no idea which genre, if any, would bring in a financial return.

Accordingly I tried my hand at everything. In three months I wrote my second novel, a 40,000 word novelette, a three-act play, and ten short stories. It wouldn't be an exaggeration to say that at times I wrote in a frenzy because to my dismay all my earlier sales of short stories had ceased. Not one had sold since our arrival in England. Almost every morning there would be a plop-plop on the carpet below the letter box as more of them came back rejected.

It was, of course, Sod's Law at work. When sales were not too important I had been able to sell them. Now that sales were essential it seemed nothing would sell.

At the same time we had to keep on trying, which was a problem in itself. To be certain the manuscripts were returned, we had to enclose return postage and the more numerous the rejections the greater the cost. Soon we wondered if we could afford to continue circulating them while at the same time knowing we would never earn any money unless we did. We were caught in a vicious circle and at times our only hope seemed to be the two full-length novels and the play I had written.

But the outlook here was just as bleak. *Laws be their Enemy* was returned from Hutchinson with the comment that it could not be considered for publication unless it was cut by at least 50,000 words. As in those days I had no knowledge of the vagaries and occasional ill-advice of publishers, I took their advice as gospel, and as the cutting would take weeks of work, *Laws* was put aside until I had finished editing my second novel.

Although time was at a premium, I was frustrated at its completion by being unable to think of a good and appropriate title. I poured through Shakespeare, The Bible, anthologies of poems, and a dozen other books without success. Then, when I felt I could afford to wait no longer and would have to use any old title, I heard a tango being played on the radio. As soon as I heard its name, *Of Masks and Faces*, something clicked in my mind. If I changed Faces to Minds, I would have a title that seemed both appropriate and intriguing.

Fired with enthusiasm again, I posted *Of Masks and Minds* to a publisher and poured my energies into the three-act play.

To my dismay *Masks* was returned five weeks later without comment. With no idea what was wrong with it, I sent it to another publisher. Before I could return to the play, our solicitor told us our petition for mother's house would be heard the following week. At the same time he warned us we would have to employ a barrister for the hearing. This was a hard blow because my parents had no capital whatever and so the cost would have to come from our rapidly dwindling kitty.

Anxious the money would not be wasted, I gave much thought to the case myself and believed I had discovered a point that ought to make our application successful. Today I've forgotten the ploy, but although my solicitor agreed it was important, he clearly took umbrage that a layman should have the temerity to brief him on the case.

The hearing itself proved a total disaster. Our barrister, whom we had not met beforehand, was not only late in arriving but stumbled

over his lines in a way that made me think he was ill until he turned and leaned over me. Then I realized he was four sheets to the wind and looked like losing our case before it was even presented.

I need not have worried too much. The English professions invariably close ranks when one of their members shows frailty, and although the magistrate's eyes were icy behind his spectacles, he adjourned the case on the grounds of our council being unwell.

I was breathing fire when I saw our solicitor later, particularly because by this time I'd discovered the barrister had a reputation for liking his whisky. My feelings weren't improved when he, the solicitor, tried to defend the 'unwell' fabrication. I told him I wanted the barrister changing and the drunken one could go and whistle for his money.

The second hearing was little better. As I expected, the case revolved around the point I had made to the solicitor but the new barrister hadn't been informed of it. As a consequence we looked like losing the case until I broke all the rules, stood up, and made the point myself. Although I gained frowns all round, it swung the balance in our favour and we were given permission to move into the house.

Although I was relieved at the verdict for my parents' sake, the muddle and general incompetence of the lawyers involved did nothing to improve my opinion of the professional classes, which had already been badly dented by my medical experiences. I was left with the belief, as firm today as it was then, that no trade or profession should be judge and jury of its own members. Only when the sealed doors are opened and the fresh breeze of public opinion is allowed to circulate around the mildewed walls can a profession keep true to its standards and its ethics.

# TWENTY-TWO

So we moved house yet again. We had lived fourteen weeks in the council house and during that time Shelagh had become pregnant again. To celebrate the occasion we had gone rash and bought ourselves a second-hand tandem bicycle for seven pounds. It had a small two-stroke engine poised over the rear wheel and when a lever was depressed on the handlebar a roller dropped on to the tyre, the engine started up, and the spinning roller aided one's pedalling.

At least it did in theory. In practice it seemed to make little difference, a thing that puzzled me. In fact, the tandem itself puzzled me because when the two of us rode it, I had to pedal harder than I had ever pedalled a cycle in my life. At first I put this down to lack of practice and the extra weight we were carrying because we strapped a cushion on the rear crossbar so that Peter could ride astride it.

But, as I had always had very strong legs, it really made no sense, and my first thought was that Shelagh behind me was not pulling her weight. When she assured me she was, I concluded she lacked the strength to do more and consoled myself that the extra exercise would do me good.

Yet the affair became absurd when one weekend I took a day off work and the three of us went into the country for a ride. On our way we came to Skidby Hill, a not too steep hill near the town of Beverley. Having struggled miles already with my thighs on fire, I had no hope of climbing it and sure enough we were no more than a quarter way up when we all fell off and sank on the grassy verge. It was an undignified moment but worse was to come. As Shelagh and I struggled for breath and Peter tinkled with laughter, a very old man on an equally aged bicycle came pedalling up the hill. He was barely breaking breath, and as he passed he gave us a glance that said a hundred things about the younger generation and none of them complimentary.

It was the final straw. That same night we visited my old RAF and Record Shop friend, Des Matthews, and poured out the story. "There's something wrong with that damned bike," I told him. "I've never known anything so hard to push."

Des, as fun loving as ever, gave Shelagh a knowing grin. "It wouldn't be someone resting her feet on the crossbar, would it?"

"That's what I thought," I said. "But she finds it as hard as I do."

"Perhaps something's jamming the wheels. Have you turned the bike upside down and spun them."

"Do you think I'm an idiot? Of course I have."

"Then could the motor roller be resting on the tyre when the motor's not firing?"

"No, I've looked at that too. I've checked everything I can think of."

Des grinned. "Then it has to be you. Civvie life is softening you up."

The old rivalry was immediately back. "I'd put a pound to a penny you couldn't push it up that hill. I'll go even further. I'll bet the two of us couldn't do it."

"The two of us? Don't talk out of your trousers, Smith."

"I mean it. It's bloody murder even on the straight."

Although by this time it was nearly midnight, the challenge had to be met. With Harry Blood, Des's cousin-in-law, riding on a single bike alongside us as a referee, Des and I set off for Skidby Hill. It took us half an hour to reach it and by that time I could hear with malicious satisfaction Des panting behind me. But nothing would make him admit his fatigue and at last the shadowy hill rose ahead of us.

"You ready?" I asked.

I noted the hoarseness of his reply. "Yes. Let's go."

We went. As fast as we could pedal we went. We went until our thighs were cracking with the strain and our lungs on fire. Yet the outcome was exactly as I had prophesied. Half the way up we wobbled from side to side and then fell in a tangled heap on the roadside.

It was a full minute before we even found the strength to swear. I lifted my sweating head. "Didn't I tell you?"

Des wasn't beaten yet. Dragging the tandem towards him, he heaved it upside down and spun the wheels. They spun round with a silkiness that mocked us. Des kicked the bike, then looked at me. "Let's try it again."

Expecting nothing less, I let him have his way. This time we weren't a quarter way up the hill before we fell off. "Had enough?" I asked.

He glared at me. "Let's try it with the motor running."

We did and we still fell off. Harry Blood was splitting his seams with laughter by this time but before we could round on him, shadowy figures loomed out of the darkness and grabbed all three of us. It seemed there were Army manoeuvres on that night and the stuttering of our motor had alerted a patrol. It took us a full fifteen minutes to convince them we weren't members of their opposing Red Force. Released at last, we made our weary way back to Des's flat and our waiting wives.

It was another two weeks before the mystery was solved and it took a cycle repair shop to solve it. The brakes were the caliper type and worked correctly when no weight was resting on the tandem. However, as soon as the cycle was mounted, the bowden cables tightened. In other words for weeks Shelagh and I had been cycling around Hull with the rear brakes almost fully on.

I don't know which of us was the more relieved, Des or myself. Our manhood had been in question and for a while it had seemed to fail the test. Now it seemed we could sleep more easily at nights again.

Pleasures, however, were at a premium that year because of the need to work but I did have one pleasant surprise just before Christmas. While we were in South Africa, a well-known literary critic named Nancy Spain had asked me if she might include a short story of mine in an anthology she was editing. Named Twelve Peaks to the Sky, it was my ghost story set on Table Mountain. Because of our present traumas I'd forgotten all about it but Shelagh had not because she bought me the recently published anthology as a Christmas present.

To me it was a lovely gift for two reasons. As Shelagh had undoubtedly intended, it was to remind me that I'd had successes in the past and they would come again. But it was also a gift of sacrifice because with the poor girl having to run our home on a ridiculously low budget I knew she would have saved up for weeks to buy it. For this reason it has always had a treasured place on my book shelf.

Although I worked seven days at week at this time we did allow ourselves the odd opportunity to see more of Johnnie Gemmell. It was in his house that we saw our first television programs. One was the Coronation, the other the famous soccer cup final at Wembley when at long last Stanley Matthews won a Cup Winners Medal.

But mostly, because he had a somewhat crotchety old mother, Johnnie would come round to see us. Chatting to him and reshaping the world had been one of the things we had missed in South Africa, and the three of us would squeeze into our tiny front bedroom and talk our heads off until well past midnight. Although seven years our senior, Johnnie had a young and imaginative mind, and he was also one of the very few people in Hull with whom I could discuss my work. This was something I was to appreciate more and more as the months went by.

# TWENTY-THREE

The new house, at the far end of Northfield Road, was no larger than our council house, and so was clearly going to cause problems when our second child was born. We were given two of the three bedrooms, the smaller one doubling up as my study before Peter was put to bed. He was due to begin school that year and, being a shy boy, he was not looking forward to it.

It was now 1953 and the first year of our two year project would soon be over. Yet despite all our efforts, the book in which I kept a list of submissions had not recorded a single sale since our return to England, although the submissions themselves now numbered hundreds.

Even worse my second novel was getting nowhere. By this time it had been rejected by seven publishers without a comment from one of them. Indeed the speed of their rejections had been discouraging in itself. In between submissions I had tried to be self-critical but however I tried I couldn't see anything fundamentally wrong with the book's structure.

In desperation I had sent it to a large London agency to test their reaction. Although their comment was non-committal enough to give no indication of the novel's quality, they had agreed to handle it, which had given me some small hope. However, by the time spring began rolling back the long northern winter, I hadn't heard a word from them for over three months and decided I could wait no longer. I would have to try publishers myself again in the hope our submissions would not clash.

This I began to do in April. I was fully aware the agency would resent this duplication of effort but I excused myself by deciding to pay them their full 10% commission should I make a sale first. I had, after all, received no replies to my three letters of enquiry and our financial position could wait no longer.

Nor did this lack of success aid our social life. Having witnessed for months the endless stream of rejected manuscripts falling from the letter box each day my mother, being as mothers are, could keep her silence no longer. Worried by the excessive hours I was working without reward, she began asking if I shouldn't look for a more practical job and do the writing in my spare time.

There was nothing I wanted to hear less. I believed, indeed I knew, that once I made such a compromise my dreams would be dead. If I found a job and money began coming in to make life easier for Shelagh, I would never find the courage or the selfishness to give in my notice a second time. It had to be now or never.

Not that I could blame my mother. For a woman who had known nothing but hardship all her life, my dream must have seemed the height of folly. Although she had been a fine pianist in her youth, her upbringing since had been commercial. Art was a hobby, a pastime, a pleasure. To make a living in this hard world one had to be practical, not a dreamer. Although he never said it, I'm certain my father thought the same, as would a million or more other Yorkshiremen.

The knowledge of all this made me frustrated and irritable and I found myself saying things that caused pain and tears. In turn this made me hate myself, which only completed the vicious circle.

Even Shelagh was now showing signs of strain. Although she never once complained, she must have been worried sick about our dwindling finances with a new baby only two months away.

All these tensions began to express themselves domestically. Although as yet only on a minor scale, they were still enough to bring back memories of our early days in South Africa. Before things reached that stage, Shelagh agreed with me that we should look for alternative accommodation before our second child was born.

Such was our state in the spring of that year. With no short stories selling and my two novels going nowhere, I decided to write a play. Calling it *The Glass Prison*, I put it into the hands of a London theatrical agent called Lawrence Fitch who lifted my spirits for a while by saying many kind things about it. Yet when spring became summer I heard nothing more from him either.

Nevertheless play writing seemed to offer the only hope in an otherwise depressing scene. By this time I had learned that young writers tend to be good at either dialogue or narrative but seldom at both. As I found I could write dialogue more quickly and easily than narrative, and as time was the essence, I decided to write a second play while I practiced writing narrative in what time was left.

In a further effort to determine where my talents lay, I decided to write a comedy play. By working on it day and night I completed it in nine weeks. Because of its unusual theme, I called it *A House Divided*.

I then sent it to Lawrence Fitch who replied to say the last act was one of the funniest he had ever read. Full of hope again, I wondered if I should concentrate on plays or risk writing a third novel.

Before making the difficult choice, I had a letter from Fitch giving me the exciting news that a London experimental theatre called the New Gateway had expressed interest in *The Glass Prison* and would like to perform it for a week during the coming autumn. Was I willing?

Was I willing!? I nearly turned cartwheels with excitement, as did Shelagh. Was this the breakthrough at last? I wanted to dash off to London right away but Fitch told me he would let me know when rehearsals began. As the trip would cost money we could ill afford, I had to be patient and force myself back to my typewriter.

But other matters were soon to take priority. In July, Shelagh was taken into the hospital at Hedon to have our second child. This time she had a painful delivery before bearing a lusty eight and a half pound boy. I spent my evenings for the next fourteen days cycling through the town on the tandem to reach the distant hospital. We juggled with names for a week and finally decided on Kevan Frederick. As with Peter, I was relieved that the child was a boy and healthy and strong with it.

As we had expected, the arrival of another child did nothing to help our accommodation problems and I was forced to spend precious time helping Shelagh to find suitable rooms. We eventually heard of a vacancy only a mile from our present flat. The house belonged to a seventy-year-old man named Mr England who did part-time work as a groundsman in the small tennis club around

*Baby Kevan*

which his house and a dozen others were grouped. It was a pleasant ambience but the factor that decided us was the rent. After Mr. England interviewed us, he said we could have the sitting room and two upstairs bedrooms for nine pounds a month. Moreover, we could use the large garden which contained over two hundred rose trees. (We learned later that between the wars the old man had worked in Kew Gardens, from which he had gained his love of roses.) With the blessing of my parents, who must have been relieved to see the back of their irritable son, we accepted his offer and moved in the following week.

Although the accommodation was ideal for us in other aspects, I soon found it difficult to work in the sitting room with a small boy and a newly-born baby in attendance. By this time I was working on a novel about the Royal Air Force. They say all writers have one novel they must get off their chest and perhaps this one was mine. I had, after all, served nearly seven years in the wartime RAF and the book was meant to be my small testament to colleagues and friends who had not survived. As I intended the book to have all the authenticity I could muster, I wrote the Air Ministry to ask if they could provide me with a suitable number. In this they were helpful. They told me that for some reason no one could explain, of the 700 squadron numbers issued, only one had not been used. If I so wished, I could use this number. This was how *633 Squadron* gained its name.

But novels are difficult things to write and with two small children in attendance and the knowledge this novel represented our last chance before total failure, I found it the hardest task yet. Moreover, it put an unfair strain on Shelagh. So, after a couple of weeks had passed, our dear old Mr England took pity on us and offered me the free use of an attic. It was chock-a-block with old furniture and had only an oil stove to provide warmth, but for me it was heaven. I could now work all day and all night if I wanted to, and would no longer be a burden on either Shelagh or the children. I moved into it with alacrity.

During this time the only relaxation we allowed ourselves was the odd game of tennis on the courts opposite. Until then we had played at the huge Hull YPI club which at the time boasted twelve hard courts, fifty grass courts, and was included in the national tennis circuit. There Shelagh had reached the final of the women's singles and only lost it because of an onset of tennis elbow. Later she had played regularly in the county league while I also managed to fit into a similar men's team. Now, although the nearby club was much smaller, it saved us a longer journey to the major venue.

Winter came before Lawrence Fitch told me that rehearsals were commencing and I could now meet the producer, the director, and the cast. Relieved and excited, I wanted to take Shelagh with me, but although my parents were willing to look after the children, Shelagh decided we could not afford two train tickets to London. So I went alone, making certain before leaving that I could stay with my brother Ray and so save accommodation expenses.

I made only one visit to the theatre and in no way can I claim it was a success. The producer and director seemed to know their business but I soon found that the semi-professional cast they had put together was as poor in pocket as I was myself. Worse, with the idea that seems endemic in the artistic world, they believed playwrights were all rich and so an easy touch for drinks after the rehearsals.

I found it more than embarrassing. I bought one round for them all, reflecting as I paid the bill that the family food for a week had just gone down ten thirsty throats, and hoped fervently that was the end of it. But as glasses were set down and anticipatory faces turned towards me again, I realized this was only my first round. Sweating, I thanked them all for their rendering of my play, stammered out some lie that my brother was expecting me back early, and then fled the theatre, never to return in spite of urgent requests until the play was performed two months later.

Before I returned home, however, my brother introduced me to his agent, Gordon Harboard, a well-known theatrical entrepreneur with offices in St. Martin's Lane. Earlier Harboard had read some of my short stories and said he would like to meet me.

So we met and he asked if he might handle my stories as he felt some were suitable for film adaptation. Yet to learn that in the art world the rosy pictures entrepreneurs paint seldom live up to the hopes they raise, I left him quite a number.

I did feel for my brother that day however. Since the illness that had ended his dancing days, he was now only obtaining 'bit' parts, and I noticed how he was virtually ignored by Harboard once I was introduced. I found myself resenting this although Ray himself made no complaint. I was learning what a cold, hard world my brother lived in but at the time I ascribed this only to the film and theatrical professions. I had yet to learn that the literary world was little better.

I made one final visit before leaving for home. It was to the literary agency who were handling *Of Masks and Minds*. I entered an imposing office but had to wait a full minute at a counter before a girl came forward to ask my business. When I told her about my novel she looked blank and moved away to whisper to a second girl. She looked equally blank and the two of them withdrew to the back of the office where they began rummaging around in a large metal cabinet. After dragging out a pile of manuscripts, the first girl showed one to her colleague. Glancing furtively around, she blew dust off its folder before coming forward and showing it to me. "Is this the one?"

I told her it was and asked where it had been sent in the months since my submission. She hesitated, then vanished from the office. On her return she looked faintly embarrassed. "I think it's been to three publishers."

I was shocked. "Only three? And you think! Don't you know?"

At that her embarrassment turned into defiance. "No, I don't. The manager who handled it is at lunch."

I glanced at my watch. It was 3.30 p.m. "When do you expect him back?"

"I don't know. He's having lunch with a client. It could be any time."

"You do know I've written three times about it and not had a single reply?"

She shrugged. "I don't suppose there was anything to tell you. We'd have written to you if we had made a sale."

I reached out for the manuscript. "Tell your manager not to bother any more. I'll handle it myself from now on."

Her shrug told me she could not have cared less. Until then I had been naive enough to believe that London-based establishments were the corps d'elite of the literary world and handled writers with both courtesy and competence. It was the first of many salutary lessons I was to learn in the years ahead.

# TWENTY-FOUR

Back home again, I sent *Of Masks and Minds* to its twelfth, or was it its thirteenth, publisher. Then I settled down to *633 Squadron* again. Fortunately I had kept most of my Air Force notes and so many of the technical facts were at my finger tips. At the same time, as the Norwegian town of Bergen featured in my book and my ultimate target was sited in a fjord, I knew that before I finished the book I would need to visit Norway. But as such a visit would heavily deplete our kitty, I pushed it to the back of my mind and devoted my time to the chapters concerning the Squadron's activities in England.

Months of work in that smoky attic followed until at last we were given a date for *The Glass Prison*. The news came as a massive tonic to me because although I believe my stamina was exceptional, no one could write for fourteen hours a day, week in and week out, without feeling the effects. To put it succinctly I was punch drunk with work and the thought of seeing my play spring into life on a London stage was the tonic I needed. We arranged for my long suffering parents to move into the house for a few days to look after the children and then took ourselves off to London.

I don't think either of us could ever forget that first night. The theatre was full but I was too nervous to see anything but the curtained stage where I believed my fate would be decided. Shelagh told me later that her knees were shaking so much she couldn't have risen from her seat had she tried.

The play was about a disparate group of patients and their visitors trapped in an Alpine sanatorium by an avalanche that could sweep over and kill them at any moment. Its theme was the contrasting reactions of those who have previously faced death through illness or war and those who had never been in a life threatening situation. It was a theme I had found rewarding in the philosophical dialogue it had offered to my characters.

I remember nothing about the broad sweep of the play. My mind was obsessed by snippets of dialogue that I had struggled over during the play's composition and as they arrived I listened intently to the reaction of the audience. I lost all awareness of time and felt in a daze when the interval came and Shelagh urged me to have a drink in the bar. In my state I needed little urging and, regardless of the cost, quickly downed two double whiskies.

At that point I didn't think anyone knew I was the author but someone must have pointed me out because a little fat man ran over to me and beamed in my face. "Remarkable!" he said. "Absolutely remarkable!"

I peered at him. "What's remarkable?"

"Your play. Its theme. Are you a doctor?"

I shook my head. "No. Why?"

"My dear fellow, then it's all the more remarkable. I wouldn't have believed that anyone, not even a doctor like myself, could have portrayed more exactly the thoughts and feelings of consumptive patients. You've got into their minds so well there were times I wanted to shout out bravo, bravo."

I didn't know what he was talking about but before I could say anything he grabbed my hand. "Well done, sir. My heartiest congratulations."

I let Shelagh steer me back into the auditorium. "Who was he?" I muttered. "What was he babbling about?"

She eased me down into my seat. "Your play, silly. Don't you know people read things into plays and novels? It happens all the time. At least you had the sense not to deny it."

The torture went on for another forty minutes. As the curtain went down I took a deep breath and waited for the boos. Instead I heard applause and for a moment wondered if it signified relief the play was over.

But no. It went on and on. The curtain kept rising and falling and then a cry went up for 'author, author'.

I never thought I'd make that stage. My legs were wobbly jelly and I had a vision of plunging ignominiously into the orchestra pit. Instead I found myself staring at a sea of faces and saying things so banal I wanted to slip down and vanish between the floorboards.

Somehow I got back to Shelagh, who was talking to a small dapper man. "Am I dreaming this or did they really like it?" I asked.

"Of course they liked it," she told me. "You had eleven curtain calls. Ask this gentleman if you don't believe me."

The small man, fortyish with thick greying hair, took my hand. He had a foreign accent I couldn't place but it seemed to fit into that unreal evening. "Congratulations, my friend. My name is Miron Grindea. Your play was full of good things. In fact I would like to talk to you about it. Will you and your charming wife come to my flat after you have said goodnight to your producer and your cast?"

I was too delirious by this time to argue. In any case, he liked my play and that was enough for me. Half an hour later we were in a taxi heading for Emperor's Gate.

I remember little about his flat except that it was stuffed with manuscripts. They were piled in corners, they bulged out of cupboards, and I seemed to remember them protruding from a trapdoor in the ceiling.

I do remember his wife, however. She was a graceful charming woman who was a concert pianist, and after a while she went out to make supper while Miron talked to us.

Although I was still too bemused to recall every snippet of that conversation, I did learn he was the editor of a prestigious Anglo-French magazine called Adam, and it didn't take me long to realize he was the most erudite man I'd so far met in London. He was a Rumanian who spoke at least half a dozen languages, and from the array of books on his shelves it seemed he could read in at least half a dozen more.

He kept filling our glasses with a delicious wine as he talked and as I sipped at it the evening became more fanciful, particularly when he told me he had found many interesting things in my play and believed I had a bright future as an author and playwright. As I listened I became more and more convinced that it was all a dream and I would soon awaken in my sooty attic to find a pile of blank sheets before me.

His last words before we left were that I must send him some of my short stories with a view to publication, and that we must look out in the next day's newspapers for the reviews which he knew would be excellent.

We bought a handful of newspapers the following day and

couldn't find a review in any of them. Bewildered, I phoned Miron to ask why. His voice was full of sympathy. Puzzled himself, he had made enquiries. It seemed some idiot at the New Gateway had not done his homework and had chosen to open the play on the very same night of a large West End opening. As a consequence every critic in London had been to the West End play and not one to mine.

In other words had *The Glass Prison* received a hundred curtain calls, it wouldn't have made the slightest difference. Club members had ensured a full house on the first night but after that only publicity would bring in the public, and of that there would be none. Aware there was no way one could fight that kind of luck, Shelagh and I took the next train home.

With my first stage venture a disaster and costing us money rather than making any, I knew I would have to work even harder in the future and in the meantime pray that one of my completed novels or even a short story would be accepted soon.

But the omens were not good. On the whole publishers took less time to make their decisions in those days and both novels seemed to be forever arriving back with printed rejection notes pinned to their covers. If their number had been added to the rejection slips sent back with my short stories, the old cliché, 'I could have papered my room with rejection slips' would have been literally true. My attic was tiny enough, and by this time my record book showed I had received over a thousand rejections without a single sale.

Thus there was every reason to believe I was the failure of failures. The two years I had given myself were drawing to a close and although I had produced a great deal of work I hadn't received one penny from it. If that didn't prove I lacked the talent to be a writer, what else did I need?

Yet somehow I did not feel a failure. I kept reading my work but couldn't see much wrong with it. This doesn't mean I wasn't self-critical. In many ways I have always suffered from a surfeit of introspection. But although I had no illusions about myself and knew I had an immense amount to learn, I still felt my work was no worse and sometimes better than many of the novels published at the time. In other words I could not extinguish a faith in myself. I still believed I could be a writer if only I had the money and the time.

But we had neither. We were now struggling along on fifteen pounds a month, which meant after the rent was paid we had thirty shillings (£1.50) a week for food and other necessities. How Shelagh managed during this time and how she refrained from asking me to get some other job or go back to South Africa I shall never know. To have faith in oneself is one thing. To have faith in another when there hasn't been a sign of success for twenty months and bills cannot be met is something else. Shelagh was quite superb.

To make things worse, that spring the Ministry of Pensions wanted to check I was still a valid case for my sixteen shillings a week pension and so I was ordered into the tropical disease hospital at Mossley Hill near Liverpool for a long series of tests. This proved a mixed blessing. It kept me from work but, if memory serves me right, we received a small weekly sum for the weeks I was away, which helped to eke out our dwindling capital.

In all I was there for six weeks in a ward full of ex-Japanese prisoners of war. During this time, in an effort to augment our capital, I was sharing a small stake with my father in the football pools. On my second weekend in the hospital I found to my intense excitement that we had scored twenty-three points out of a maximum twenty-four on the eight draws column. As one of the men in my ward had a wife who worked in the pools company, I asked him to find out what the dividend would be, and he told me it would be well over three thousand pounds.

Three thousand pounds! Our troubles were over at last! I could write forever! As we weren't confined to bed between our medical tests, I asked for permission to go home for a day or two.

I was given it and arrived on the Sunday night. With Shelagh and my parents as excited as I was, we all went out to celebrate. I was still celebrating when I returned to the hospital on Tuesday morning.

But not for long. On my arrival my pools informant came over to me looking embarrassed and contrite. "Sorry, mate, but as you probably know by this time my wife made a mistake. There were dozens of draws last week and the divided sum for twenty-three points is only twelve and sixpence."

Twelve and sixpence! Split between my father and myself that was six shillings and threepence each. I had spent more than that on the train fare. I won't attempt to describe my feelings. One is left either to cry or to break into laughter at fate's sense of humour. I can't remember which choice I made.

But there were compensations as there usually are. Because our ward had Japanese prisoners of war connections, the girls at one of the large football pool syndicates adopted us and took us out on a few occasions, once to see the Grand National. In some ways, with the mordant jokes that flew around the ward, it was like being in the Services again, and so less depressing than being in a general hospital.

As always, however, my case had to be different. After a series of general X-rays, I kept being sent back for more X-rays of my neck. My protests that I was there for bowel investigations were ignored and my neck received all the attention until one day I was called in front of our ward doctor, whom we were told was Polish. He came to the point right away. "When did you fracture your neck?"

I stared at him. "I've never fractured my neck. You must have got the wrong man."

In all military pension investigations, it seems every statement a man makes is suspect. His frown deepened. "You are Frederick Escreet Smith?"

"Yes, I am."

"Then we haven't got the wrong man. Why won't you tell me about the fracture?"

"Because I haven't had a fracture. What else can I say?"

"You are not telling the truth. What do you expect to gain by it?"

My own temper was fraying now. "I'm not expecting to gain anything. Nor am I lying. I'm here to have my bowels checked. So what's all this nonsense about my neck?"

He was a choleric character and was now showing anger. Equally my Mr Hyde was resenting being treated as if I was still in the Services. No doubt the heat in the office was another factor because the sun was shining through the glass and falling on a row of bottles that lined the window ledge. As we began snapping at one another, there was a sudden loud plop as a cork shot out of one of the heated bottles.

I don't know why but it made me laugh. He stared at me as if he now thought I was a case for the psychiatrists. "What are you laughing at?"

"I don't know," I managed. "Perhaps it's because I find my treatment here a farce."

He said something then made a gesture of dismissal. As I reached the door he made his parting shot. "We'll find out how you fractured your neck if it's the last thing we do."

Perhaps because I had never imagined the injury could have been so serious, I was back in the ward before I remembered my incident with the Heinkel in East Anglia. So that was why I had known such pain in my head and neck over the years. Could my neck really have been fractured?

I made mention of it the next time I had X-rays and they confirmed a fracture that had over the months healed itself. At the same time they warned me that the resultant nodule would cause me problems and pain in the years ahead. Even so, I never received an additional pension for the injury. Perhaps my altercation with the doctor was the reason.

I had no more satisfaction with my amoebic dysentery. After six weeks I was told no traces of it could be found and so I was offered sixty pounds to terminate my pension. Although I was still suffering painful attacks and have suffered them ever since, I knew the negative tests would almost certainly end my small pension and so I cashed in my losses and accepted the sixty pounds. At least, I thought, it would give us a few more months of survival.

## TWENTY-FIVE

Back home, Peter had now started school. Like my father in past years taking me to Craven Street, I had taken Peter on his first morning, and like my father I needed a stiff drink after I left him there. For although the school proved to be educationally sound, it had a high percentage of tough kids, and because Peter spoke differently to them, he was immediately singled out for bullying.

*Peter (in school cap) with Kevan*

I remember vividly the day when he confessed how boys had shoved and struck him. He was less upset than bewildered. Why had they done it, he asked. He hadn't done anything to them. Why did they behave this way?

It was one of those days when being a father is a kind of penance. You want your son to stay a gentle, caring person because you know such people are the salt of the earth and you want them to stay that way. At the same time your life has taught you that if meekness allows itself to perish, the world will become a living hell.

So I had to teach my son to fight while at the same time to impress on him he must never use such knowledge except in self defence. In the lessons that followed he had to hit me and it made him cry to do this. But I had to grit my teeth and make him do it. At the end of it I don't know who was the more upset. I could only hope that I was right and, even if I wasn't, that one day he would understand and forgive me.

My mother was very good to Peter at this time. Because he had developed a love of trains, she would often come round after school and take him to the local railway station where she would spend hours with him, often in extremely adverse conditions. During these visits she often brought us little gifts of food. We usually accepted them because it would have been ungracious to have done anything else but we didn't encourage her. We knew how little they had themselves.

Other help came from an unexpected quarter. Ray wrote to say he was now working as a supervisor at the Battersea Pleasure Gardens and one of his staff had fallen ill. The man expected to be off sick for a month and if I would like the job, Ray believed he could keep it open for me. But I must come at once. If I wished I could bring the family because there was room in his new flat at Camberwell.

As it was only a temporary job, I felt it was one I could safely take. So the very next day, with Kevan in a carry cot, we took the train again for London.

It was the beginning of three hilarious weeks. Battersea Gardens were having a festival and the huge grounds were filled with bandstands, pavilions, showmen, and exotic man-made caves full of witches, hobgoblins, and creatures from Disney cartoons.

My job was the turnstile operator on one of these artificial caves called The Grotto. I would begin at 11 a.m. and work through until 9 p.m. The hours were long but to me, used to the confinement of the attic, they were full of interest and incident. Moreover, they filled my mind with new ideas. Every evening two acrobats, a man and a woman, would shin up two high metal poles positioned fifty yards from the Grotto entrance. Once at the top, precariously standing on tiny platforms, the couple would begin to sway the fifty foot poles until their oscillations made brief contact. In that fraction of a second the acrobats would change platforms before plunging dizzily away again.

It was a hair-raising act that was performed every night during my weeks on the Grotto and I noted every detail carefully. I felt certain I could weave an exciting short story around the performance, and this I was to do on my return.

However, my job itself wasn't without incident either. The turnstile in front of my booth must have been designed by a particularly slim character because I, who have always had narrow hips, could only just pass comfortably through it. For the average plump East End women who were flocking to the festival, it was a non-starter from the beginning.

There was an escape entrance at the opposite side of the turnstile but using it meant an admission of obesity. Most plump women accepted their limitations with good grace and made a joke of it, but there were always one or two, usually those accompanied by a boy friend, who saw the turnstile as a challenge and would take it on.

The results were often hilarious. One buxom, heavily-made-up woman, as broad as she was tall, and with a gaudily dressed man behind her, grasped the metal barrier as if it was an enemy that had to be conquered,

Fearing the worst, I pleaded with her. "You can go round the turnstile if you wish, madam."

She stared at me. "Why should I?"

I could see it was a moment that called for tact. "I just thought it might be easier for you, that's all."

"Why the 'ell should it be easier?"

I gave a helpless gesture. "I don't know. Go which way you like, madam. I don't mind."

The man behind her met my eye and gave me a wink. The woman glared at me and then heaved herself forward. The turnstile groaned and then jammed solid, with one metal support in front of her and the other jammed against her bottom. She struggled but nothing moved. She was as tight as a cork in a bottle. Face perspiring and incensed, she turned to me. "Get me out! Move the bloody thing!"

I struggled with levers but nothing gave. "I can't. You've jammed it."

She tried to turn towards her companion. "Don't just stand there, you git. Help me."

He put two arms around her waist and pulled but nothing happened. By this time the woman's profanity was bringing up a grinning crowd. Advice came thick and fast. "Chop six inches off her arse," someone shouted. "Blow 'er up and float 'er out," another wit suggested.

Unable to help from the booth, I ran out and tried to pull back the turnstile. But it must have been driven off its cogs because it wouldn't move an inch. By this time the woman was hysterical and her language something to wonder at. Not daring to leave the day's takings unattended, I had to go back into the booth and empty it all into my pockets. Then, clanking like the metal man in the Wizard of Oz, I ran off to find a mechanic.

It was fifteen minutes before I found one and by this time hundreds of people had gathered. From their comments it was the best act of the day. We fought our way through them and the mechanic began to dismantle the mechanism. It took another quarter of an hour before the turnstile gave way and the woman staggered free to a great cheer from the crowd.

When she recovered I thought she was going to attack me. She shook her fist and screamed obscenities while I took cover in the booth. When at last her boy friend persuaded her to leave, she was followed to the gates by the laughing, cheering crowd. With the belief that a man should always learn from his mishaps, I wouldn't let the mechanic leave until he had fixed the turnstile so I could free it myself if the worst happened again. Fortunately it never did.

Although with a baby to look after Shelagh could do little during my working days, we did manage some sightseeing on my three off-duty afternoons. As it was now summer we managed a couple of visits to the London parks and one day, rash with a week's wages in our pockets, we took Peter and Kevan to the Zoo.

With no car for transport, we had to manhandle Kevan in his carry cot, and walking round parks and taking buses was no easy task. It seemed in those days that even pleasure was hard work and on each of our three trips we arrived back at Ray's flat tired out. But at least Peter had enjoyed his outings, and as Ray would take no money for our food and shelter, we were eventually able to return to Hull fifteen pounds better off than when we left.

As that gave me an extra month to write, we felt the trip had been a success, although it was marred to some extent on our arrival home when we found a pile of rejected manuscripts awaiting us, and some of the precious money had to be spent sending them out again. By this time *Of Mask and Minds* had been to fifteen publishers and even I was beginning to wonder if the money invested in its submissions was worthwhile.

All too soon we were on the penultimate month of our project. When we paid our rent and set aside money for food and bills, we had just six shillings and eight pence (35p) left in our bank account. The amount is burned in my brain because it meant we would have to sell our only means of transport, the tandem, if we were to survive a further month. By this time, having spent our return fare, we had both abandoned any thought of returning to South Africa. Survival was now the name of the game and survival occupied our thoughts day and night.

## TWENTY-SIX

The tandem sale was made but the nine pounds received only served to pay the rent and our deadline was almost upon us. In less than two weeks we would be totally out of money. On a survival scale it was not disaster because I could always seek work as a clerk or a labourer but it did mean my dream of being a writer would be finally over. As a consequence they were days of darkness for me because on every count it seemed I had failed.

Then a thing happened that was both electric and frustrating. On my sixteenth submission the publishers Hutchinson returned *Of Masks and Minds* with a dossier and a long covering letter. The gist of the letter was that their readers had found the novel interesting and even exciting but they had expressed doubts about its medical details on which the story was based. Accordingly, the manuscript had been sent to a consultant psychiatrist who had sent back the enclosed dossier listing its errors. If I could amend these errors, Hutchinson would give the novel further consideration.

My excitement turned into frustration when I read the dossier. To make the many amendments it suggested would totally destroy the story line and leave it with characters devoid of aim or purpose. In other words I would have no novel left. Even in that moment of intense disappointment, I remember feeling astonished that a publisher had not realized this and given me such futile and tantalising advice.

I think this was my worst frustration to date. To be so near after two years of disappointments and yet so far was so much worse than a simple rejection.

For two days I paced about wondering what I should do. It was a Tantalus and the Grapes situation and the more I struggled to find an answer, the worse my frustration grew. Finally I decided desperate situations call for desperate measures. I had little or no hope that my action would solve the problem but I couldn't find it in myself to write back to Hutchinson and destroy my last chance of success.

So I did a bizarre thing, an act totally out of character. I obtained a list of the psychiatrists in the city, closed my eyes, and jabbed down on the names with a pin. Opening my eyes, I saw the pin had come down opposite a Dr John MacKay. Not daring to think I then went to the nearest phone box and dialled his number.

I fully expected a receptionist to answer and that my request would be pushed perfunctorily aside. Instead a brusque Scots voice asked me my business.

This was the beginning of what I have always unashamedly called my miracle. By pure luck I found myself speaking to the doctor himself and to my relief he remained patient while I blabbed out my problem. "I know I am asking a great deal of you but will you consider giving me your advice? Without it I don't know what to do and my situation is more than urgent."

I don't know what I expected but to my disbelief he told me to visit him after surgery that evening and bring both my novel and the medical dossier. My feelings as I put the phone down were confused. I felt MacKay must agree with the other psychiatrist's opinion and so no real gain would be made. Yet on the other hand I would know that I had done everything in my power to avoid the novel's ultimate rejection.

MacKay was waiting for me when I arrived at his home that evening. He was a stockily-built Scot with a rugged face, heavy eyebrows, and a somewhat bluff manner. Aware of my audacity, I found him slightly intimidating when he told me to sit down and tell him the full story.

This I did and he interrupted me only twice with questions. When I finished, hoping I had not sounded too melodramatic or woebegone, he told me to leave my novel and the dossier on his desk. He would read them over the weekend and if I came back on Monday I would receive his opinion.

I returned on the Monday with few if any expectations. After all, I had every reason to believe one psychiatrist would think the same way as another. But at least I had stopped feeling sorry for myself and felt that was progress of a kind.

I imagined MacKay's attitude was more sympathetic than it had been the previous week, but I attributed that to the disappointing news he was about to give me. "Now, laddie, pull up a chair while we have a wee chat about your novel."

I couldn't contain my nervousness. "Did you get a chance to read it?"

I could have sworn his eyes twinkled under their bushy eyebrows. "Aye, I did. And so did my wife."

I showed surprise. "She has read it too?"

"Aye, as much as she could. She looked at it while I was reading the psychiatrist's report."

Here it comes, I thought. "They've really damned the novel, haven't they?"

He lifted a hand. "Hang on. One thing at a time. I liked your novel. It's fresh and it's full of interesting ideas. My wife thought the same."

That at least was gratifying. "Thank you. But how can I make the changes they want? They would kill the story stone dead."

"They certainly would, laddie. But maybe you won't need to."

For a moment I wasn't with him. Then my eyes shot wide open. "Are you saying you don't agree with the complaints?"

His eyes twinkled again at my eagerness. "Aye, I am. I can't find a thing wrong with your novel. I've just told you. It's fresh and full of interesting ideas."

I took a deep, disbelieving breath. "Then would you consider writing a letter telling that to Hutchinson? It might make all the difference."

He reached in a drawer and handed me an envelope. "I already have, laddie. Send this back to them with your manuscript and let's see what happens."

Hardly daring to believe him, I did as he suggested and the novel was accepted without a single technical element changed. My generous, warm-hearted benefactor had saved the day for us.

I have to class it as a miracle, particularly when I learned later that MacKay had a medical interest in the minds of artists and writers, and my blind jab of the pin had linked me with him. Any other psychiatrist would in all likelihood have dismissed my case as unworthy of his attention.

So it was on the last minute to midnight that our hopes were realized. I received a contract from Hutchinson that entitled me to receive £35 on signature and a further £35 on publication of the book the following year. Small although the payment was, to us it represented a massive break through that meant we could not only subsist for another few months but it also renewed my hope that I did have the qualifications to be a professional writer.

Huge relief though it was, I think Shelagh's delight was my greatest reward. For years she had lived a life that not one woman in a thousand would have suffered, and at last her faith was being rewarded. It made me wonder if there is a kind of cosmic justice present in the world. If one tries hard enough — and I believe I had done that — and if one refuses to allow disappointments or defeat to break one's spirit — does a moment come when life relents and allows one victory? I believe this is true and never once since that meeting with Dr MacKay have I ever allowed myself to even contemplate failure.

My contract with Hutchinson had its usual clause of an option on my next novel and here, with *Laws be their Enemy* completed, I was in a position to supply one, although the original copy was dog-eared from its many rejections. With Shelagh's help I touched up its worst pages, gave it a new cover, and then sent it off to my Hutchinson editor named Raymond Anderson.

I can't say I felt no anxiety while waiting for a reply. Like *Masks*, *Laws* had been rejected many times and I was still to learn how suspect the opinions of publishers can be. I was also worried that Anderson might guess that the quick dispatch of the second novel meant it had already been to other publishers.

I need not have worried. He liked it very much and suggested that I came down to London to meet him.

This I did and when we talked over lunch I found we had many views and ideas in common. I also discovered, unlike some editors I was to meet later, that he loved books and had a huge library of his own. To my gratification he told me he liked my work and hoped we would have a long and happy association. By the time we had finished a bottle of wine, I floated rather than walked from the restaurant. After two years in the doghouse, all this praise was heady stuff indeed. In addition the war had taught me enough about men to feel confident his words were sincere.

Back in his office I was introduced to his Subsidiary Rights Manager whose name I have forgotten. He was a man in his late twenties, with the confidence that public schools impart and which so often clashes with the Northerner's dislike of self-esteem. I think we both felt this imbalance of personalities from the outset and in my case it was not to diminish in the days ahead. At the time, however, I consoled myself with the instinctive feeling that Anderson was not too fond of him either.

He, the Rights Manager, informed me that he was negotiating the serial rights of *Of Masks and Minds* with various magazines and would be in touch with me if and when he had any news. All this would have been pleasing enough if he hadn't made it clear by his behaviour that I was only a young writer, a mere minnow in the organization, and I should be content with anything he obtained for me.

In truth, of course, the contracts I received for the two novels were not generous but as Hutchinson were the first publisher I had dealt with, I did not know this. Like so many other young writers without agents, my need to be published did not allow me to argue over publisher's terms.

All this I learned later. At the time I was only too pleased to hear that my second novel was accepted, particularly because this time I was to receive the princely sum of £120, although once again split into two halves. With *Masks* due to be published in the autumn of 1954, the road to stardom seemed just over the hill.

So I returned to my attic and *633 Squadron* full of optimism. I knew now I would be able to afford to visit Norway when the time came and before that we could afford a few luxuries, play some tennis, and perhaps take a short holiday. Life seemed full of promise again, particularly when an excellent foreign rights agent I acquired, called Laura Sagar, began to sell some of my short stories both in England and Scandinavia. The money was only small but nevertheless the stories were ones that had already been rejected time and again by numerous magazines. I tried to make sense of it all but could not. I would have to accept that I was in a profession that denied all logic and commonsense: a conclusion I have no reason to dispute to this day.

My excitement was growing as the publication date of *Masks* grew nearer, although it received a setback when Raymond Anderson suggested that I go round the local bookshops to make myself known and to encourage the shops to stock up with copies. They might, he suggested, even lay on a book signing session for me on publication day!

Although I had always found it difficult to promote myself, I felt I ought to do as he asked and so spent a day going round the city.

It proved a salutary experience and taught me how little London editors know about Northerners and their psychology. If I was greeted with a yawn on my confession that I was the author of a forthcoming novel, the yawn turned into a loveless frown on mention that I lived locally. My publishers, I was told, must be joking if they expected a book signing session. Didn't they know how difficult it was to sell books by local authors? Didn't I know it myself, if it came to that?

It took me some time to work this out. Why did local authors carry this mark of Cain? What was there about us that made us so different from the high-fliers in London?

The truth came to me when I remembered my experience in athletics when a teenager. The North had suffered so long from Southern indifference that it had developed a psychology of its own. With London claiming the seat of power in the arts world, an equation had been reached. The North would cling to its macho image and its virility and the South could keep all the artists. Who gave a sod about those sissies anyway?

In other words, in Hull and in other northern cities at that time, the words local author were the kiss of death. For the first time I realised why writers like J.B. Priestley had been forced to emigrate south.

Nevertheless, my excitement and expectations for *Masks*

remained high and were nearly at fever pitch when it was published as a hardcover on the 15th September at a price of nine shillings and sixpence. In anticipation I had gone to stay in London at my brother's flat and I remember my thoughts when I awoke that morning.

This was my day. The morning when every bookshop in London and indeed in England would have my book in its window. Every newspaper of any import would contain a review. I was at the entrance of fame and fortune. The days of poverty and disappointment were over.

I couldn't wait for the bookshops to open. Helped geographically by my brother, I hurried to the nearest one and was shocked to find no trace of my book in the window. When I went inside and asked the manager the reason, he told me he'd never heard of *Of Masks and Minds*. Nor did his ignorance seem to cause him the slightest concern. Deciding he was a manager without discernment, I hurried on to the next shop only to discover again that my novel was neither present nor known.

Helped by my brother we searched all day and found only six books in the entire city, and they were in Hatchards. Even this could hardly be hailed as a triumph because Hatchards claimed they stocked copies of every book that was published. My brother bought one to aid sales and then we returned to his flat. My great day was over and I was left with the feeling that no matter how many books I sold in the future, publication days would never hold quite the same excitement for me again. After what had happened, it was not a thought to savour.

## TWENTY-SEVEN

Although my disappointment over the initial appearance of *Masks* left its mark, I did have some recompense in the months that followed. The Rights Manager of Hutchinson had asked me for the names of any magazines who had published previous work of mine and I had mentioned the South African magazine Outspan. He must have sent them a copy of the book because in November I received the news that Outspan would be featuring the novel as a serial in their special Christmas edition. Their payment was £150, more than I had received from the Hutchinson book sale.

By this time I had also received newspaper reviews and although most were only one or two column inches, nearly all were excellent. When one or two suggested I was a new writer of promise, and when both Dutch and Danish book translations were sold, my puzzlement grew why fifteen publishers had previously turned the novel down.

Around Christmas or early in the New Year, the Hutchinson Rights Manager told me, with considerable self-gratification, that he had sold the film rights of *Masks* to a man called Emmett Dalton. Although I believe Dalton owned or had a share in a small Irish film studio, he was not intending to make the film himself. He was acting as a middle man who bought film rights of likely novels for small figures and sold them for much greater ones to interested larger film companies. In this case I was to receive £450 less 25% which Hutchinson took as their agency commission.

Although the going rate for film rights even in those days ran into thousands of pounds, it was not the smallness of the offer that upset me. It was the tone of the letters from the self-opinionated young man who was handling my work. In spite of the interest and sales *Masks* was receiving, his letters made it clear he saw me as a second or third rate author who should be grateful for the sales he was getting me. Perhaps I was being over sensitive but his general behaviour was in marked contrast to that of his editor Raymond Anderson.

However, after our earlier impecunious days, it was money and enabled us to buy much needed clothes for ourselves and the two children. It also meant I could now afford to travel to Norway to complete *633 Squadron* but first I had to wait until *Laws be their Enemy* was published.

It was now an event occurred that was to put another dent in my one-time idealistic view of the world of art and literature. Conscious I had written a relatively successful play in *The Glass Prison* in spite of all that had happened, I decided to try for the broadcast media. Accordingly I made a few alterations to my second play and posted off the manuscript.

Six weeks passed and then we received a letter from a play producer. My play interested him and he would like to meet me. If it were convenient, he would visit us the following week.

Greatly excited, we made provision for his visit, even to the extravagance of a bottle of wine. Our producer duly arrived and confused us by talking for the next ninety minutes about almost anything but my play. Uncertain how to handle such negotiations, I waited almost until he was leaving before mentioning it.

"Ah, yes, the play," he said. "Don't worry about it. Everything is in hand and I will be getting in touch with you shortly." With that and a bright smile, he climbed into the taxi he had ordered and drove away.

We were left bemused and bewildered. What on earth had he travelled all that way for? We found out a few weeks later. A local friend who had read my play came round and told us how much she had enjoyed its production, although she couldn't understand why some of its events had been slightly altered and the names of the characters changed. Another friend wrote to say much the same. He also asked why another name than mine had been given credit for the story.

Having not heard the play, we were puzzled until the truth sank in. Our friendly producer had come with no intention of negotiating it even if he possessed the means. He had come to see if we had the money for litigation if he or a friend plagiarized it. When he had seen our stringent circumstances, he knew he was safe to go ahead.

He was right. There was nothing we could do against the

organization behind him, although I am absolutely certain they knew nothing whatever about his deceit. As an independent producer, he must have given my manuscript to a friend who, after copying my theme, story line and structure, had made a few cosmetic changes and then sent the result in as an original work. After it was accepted the two conspirators would have shared the spoils. Thus rogues prosper and their victims begin to lose faith in a profession they had once admired and respected.

Pop, Shelagh's father, arrived in the spring. Although of Irish descent, he had never been to the land of his fathers and the purpose of his trip was to pay a visit there. He was also eager to see his younger daughter, and Peter, and Kevan, the latter who had been born in England.

Now in his autumnal years, Pop was a friendly, placid man who brought no stress into a household and we were glad to see him, although accommodation was a problem because, being still with Mr England, we had only two bedrooms. However, by moving Peter's bed into our room, we were able to manage reasonably well. He quickly made friends in our local pub but from our talks we knew he saw Eire as his real goal, a magic isle of mountains, St Patrick and leprechauns. His anticipation of his visit was both moving and infectious.

But how different was his mood on his return two weeks later. He barely made mention of his trip, and when we tentatively asked if he had enjoyed himself, he made non-committal remarks and changed the subject.

It was a full week before we discovered the reason. He had arrived at the docks full of eagerness for his first contact with Ireland, and the first born-and-bred Irishman he had encountered had been a taxi driver. Firstly the man had ignored his request to help him with his suitcases. Then he had been rudeness itself when Pop had tried to talk to him during the journey. But the coup de grace had been the fee he had demanded when Pop reached his hotel. Realizing by this time that Pop was from overseas, he had tried to extract from him an exorbitant fare.

Although a placid man, Pop, who had won amateur boxing titles in his youth, was no push-over and in the ding-dong that followed, he had almost come to blows with the driver. Eventually the affair had been settled by his paying half the illegal fare but the discord had left its mark. Although the rest of the trip had gone well enough and he had met many friendly and warm-hearted people, Pop confessed one night after a couple of drinks that this one incident had somehow soiled the dreams of a lifetime.

I remember feeling very sorry for him and making myself a secret pledge. If first impressions are so important — and they do seem to be — then I for one would always try to be pleasant to any foreigner who was new to one's country. The power to create an anglophobe or an anglophile might well depend on that first vital communion. I hope Customs Officials, Immigration Officers, and taxi drivers everywhere take careful note.

With Pop hiring a caravan for the five of us, we took a short holiday in Devon that year. Why we chose June I can't think because Laws was published while we were away and I should have been available had the publishers needed me. I can only think the publication date was changed and caught me by surprise.

Whatever the reason, it was an unfortunate clash of interests and made worse by a sudden rail strike. This not only made it difficult for us to get back home but, far worse, it became difficult if not impossible for the publishers to distribute the book around the country. It was my first but by no means last experience of how strikes can damage and even destroy years of painstaking work.

On the holiday side, however, we were blessed with good weather. It was so hot that Shelagh had a slight touch of sunstroke, which brought amused comments from both Pop and me. As we hadn't a car, most of our time was spent on the beach, but in such fine weather this was no hardship and the children enjoyed themselves.

Our only outing was a bus ride to Clovelly where we climbed down the steep incline to the beach. As Kevan was barely two years old, he had the privilege of being carried down in his push chair.

*L.toR:
Kevan,
Peter,
and Pop*

*The Boys
(L.toR. Kevan, Peter),
Shelagh (in hat),
Shelagh's mother
(Mrs. McKay)
in front.*

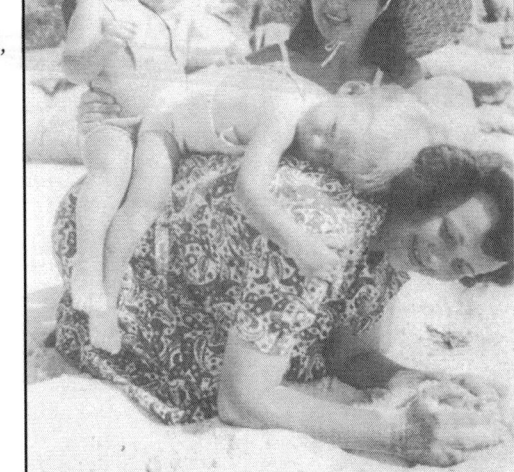

Around that time he was going through one of those infantile spells that make life difficult for parents and relations alike. At home he would stand up in his cot at nights, grab the bars, and shake the entire structure until in our lounge below it sounded like overhead thunder. Later, when we crept into bed, he would feign sleep until we had reached that critical point between wakefulness and slumber when the psyche is vulnerable. Then he would let out a single piercing cry that would bring us bolt upright with pounding hearts.

Given attention he would show no sign of pain and would seem to fall asleep as soon he was returned to his cot. Yet more often than not, he would repeat the performance just as we were drifting off to sleep again. Shelagh bore it with her usual equanimity but there were times when I was less patient.

Like many other children, Kevan, who only a few years later was to become one of the most lovable and generous teenagers one could wish for, had a favorite toy, a Teddy bear. Teddy, who had only one eye, would be cuddled in his arms one day and then hurled away the next as if it had suddenly become his worse enemy. It was such a day when we went to Clovelly. Down the steep incline to the beach he had kept throwing Teddy out of his push chair and no doubt gleefully watched the three of us finding and picking it up. But on this day it seemed Teddy might have had enough punishment because after we spent a couple of hours on the beach and were carrying Kevan up to the top road, there was a sudden cry from the young tyrant. Where was One-Eyed Teddy? Where had he gone?

Teddy had vanished and for us it was panic stations. Without him present in Kevan's cot at nights, sleep would be a thing of the past. Peter offered to go down to look for him but with our bus due in minutes and a three hour wait for the next, it was clearly a job for the man of the house. So down the steps I went like a mountain goat, searching for One-Eye as I went.

It was no easy task. In his current mood our little tyrant could hurl Teddy away with the force of an Olympic athlete. Seeing nothing of Teddy on my way down, my instinct told me where he would be.

Instinct proved me right. Teddy was taking cover under a fishing boat near where we had spent the last two hours. Grabbing him I raced back to the steps, conscious I had only three minutes left if we were to catch the bus.

Up I went, with legs aching and lungs burning. As I reached the top, Shelagh gave a sigh of relief when she saw Teddy was safe in my sweating hands. At the same moment Kevan gave a cry and held out his chubby arms. "Teddy! I want my Teddy!"

I rammed the furry creature into his push chair. "Don't you ever throw him away again," I hissed. "If you do, he'll never come back."

I received a hurt glance. "Kevan doesn't throw Teddy away. Kevan loves Teddy."

"Don't give me that, you little phoney. You're always throwing him away and he's had enough."

Pop and Peter climbed into the bus. Jumping on the step I helped Shelagh lift up the push chair. As the conductor rang the bell and we turned to find a seat, Kevan let out a cry. "Teddy's gone. I want my Teddy."

I knew where Teddy was before I rang the stop bell. Apologizing to the conductor, I jumped off the bus and ran back along the road. With the skill born of practice, our little tyrant had hurled Teddy away even as we were climbing aboard.

When I picked Teddy up, with his one eye gummed up with oil, his expression said it all. "Give me to someone else. Please, please, please!" But when I heard muffled cries coming from the bus calling for him I knew I lacked the courage. At the same time, when I jumped back on the bus and handed Teddy back to his cherubic oppressor, I am certain Teddy was crying.

# TWENTY-EIGHT

On our return home, Hutchinson asked me to go round the local book shops to promote *Laws*. Although not looking forward to the task, I agreed because by this time some of the reviews were out and although as yet they were mostly from provincial newspapers, they were very good. The ones from the quality papers hadn't yet been sent in by the news cutting services but I had no reason to believe they would be any different.

So I was totally unprepared for what happened that morning. Going into Colletts, one of a chain of left-wing bookshops, I told the girl about my novel and asked if I might speak to the manager. She gave me a disinterested look and then disappeared into a rear room.

The disinterested look was something I had expected from my experience with *Of Masks and Minds*. What I didn't expect was the attack of the little man who burst out into the shop a couple of minutes later. "How dare you come in here touting your disgusting book?"

I stood there half stunned. "Disgusting?"

"Yes. I wouldn't stock the thing if it were the last book on earth. You ought to be ashamed of yourself."

I didn't know what to say. "You are talking about my book? *Laws be their Enemy*?"

"Of course I'm talking about your bloody book. I can't stand you people who disguise trash with high-sounding titles. At least you could be honest and let people know the rubbish you've written."

What does a writer say under an attack like that? I backed towards the door. "I'm sorry you don't like it. I thought I'd painted a fair picture of how things are over in South Africa."

His anger rose to new heights. "A fair picture? Putting in all that sentimental trash when millions of poor devils are starving or dying of consumption. What's the matter with you? Don't you have any feeling or social conscience? For that matter, what's wrong with your publishers? What are they doing wasting money and paper on you when the world's full of wrongs that need exposing."

I was shattered. I turned and fled for home. Until then I had kept sneaking glances at my courtesy copy of the book and enjoyed the feel of it in my hands. Because of the huge effort that goes into writing a novel, the initial sight of the published version is often the first real pleasure a writer gets from his work. But after my Colletts' experience, even this pleasure was denied me. I found myself dreading the arrival of my quality newspaper reviews.

It was all explained three days later. One of the newspapers — I'm not certain which although it might have been the Times Literary Supplement — had by mistake crossed the title of my book with a light romance based superficially on apartheid. My Colletts' manager had been rightly disgusted that such a serious subject had been made the vehicle for a trivial love story.

Although the rest of my reviews were excellent, it was my last visit to a bookshop about that novel. Indeed, I can count on the fingers of one hand the times I have visited bookshops about my novels since. In some way that experience bruised me so much that I have preferred to stay home and let nature take its course.

With Shelagh telling me she was happy enough to take care of the children during my absence, I took my short trip to Norway shortly afterwards. My brief was to find a suitable fjord in which to site my target and to plot my air attacks on the city of Bergen.

My problem was still money because the foreign sales of book and serial rights, welcome though they had been, had only brought in a few hundred pounds. As for *Laws*, in spite of the two years work it had taken to research and write, it brought in nothing more than its original advance of £120. In a way this did not surprise me because I think I had already realized that serious novels were not often lucrative ones.

At the same time, even if the money return didn't disappoint me, I would have liked the book to have reached a greater audience than a single English hardcover copy could obtain. But it soon became clear that few people in Britain, Europe, or America for that matter, gave much thought to apartheid in the Fifties. That concern was to come much later. It was not the first time in my writing life, and by no means the last, that I had jumped the gun and paid for it.

As a result of all this, my ship journey from Newcastle to Bergen was all we could legitimately afford and the rest would have to be done on a shoestring. Accordingly I asked Mr England if I might borrow his bicycle. It was extremely old with high, narrow handlebars, and I felt like Grandfather Greybeard when riding it, but pride had to give way to expediency. I felt it ought to save me travel expenses while I was over there and that was all that mattered. For accommodation I planned to stay in Youth Hostels.

Aware I might also have to do a great deal of walking, I decided to toughen up my feet and spent two weekends doing lengthy walks. One of these was from Bridlington to Scarborough and back, a total distance of around fifty miles.

I completed the first leg satisfactorily, stayed the night in a hostel, and started back on the Sunday. By the time I had covered twelve miles, I had developed a huge blister that was growing larger by the minute. As I hobbled down a winding road, an old car full of young men swung round a corner and made straight for me, the joke presumably to make me jump for my life. This I did, only to land with my blister on a brick half hidden on the grassy verge.

As my foot exploded in pain, I discovered Mr Hyde had not abandoned me, as I had often hoped, but had only been in hibernation. Letting out a roar of fury, he leapt up, seized the brick, and hurled it after the car. It went like a bullet and struck and cracked the rear window.

Tyres squealed as the car halted and three angry youths leapt out. 'No doubt they expected to see me run which was the only sensible thing to do, but Mr Hyde had no such intentions. With another howl of fury he began running headlong at the youths who took one look at him and dived back into their car. A moment later they disappeared round a corner in a cloud of oily smoke.

Sweating, I sank down on the grass. I knew if Hyde had caught them, there would have been no Norway next month for me. In all likelihood I would have spent it in prison.

My ten days in Norway were full of interest. Prior to going, I had asked their Tourist Board for contacts and they had put me in touch with the literary reviewer of the local newspaper, the Bergen Tidende, and he and his wife not only met me at the quayside but were to prove both hospitable and helpful in the days ahead.

As my first task was to reconnoitre Bergen, I spent my first two days up Floien mountain which provided a bird's eye view of the city. I also stayed in the Youth Hostel which was sited near the funicular on the crest of the mountain.

All went well the first day when I took photographs of the city. But on the second day, while I was planning and sketching attack routes for my aircraft, I felt a tap on my shoulder and found three burly policemen standing over me. Someone had informed the police about my activities and as the Cold War was particularly frigid at the time, I was thought to be a Russian spy. As I couldn't speak Norwegian and my police escort couldn't speak English, it was a full eight hours before I could establish my credentials and obtain my release from the local police station.

My next step was to find a suitable fjord in which to set my target. I wanted one that would pose problems for attacking aircraft and was advised to try the Gudvangen Fjord some forty miles from Bergen. Finding the old bicycle totally unsuited for the steep and winding roads, I was forced to take a bus to the fjord.

I found it impressive and spectacular, with sides so precipitous that waterfalls broke into rainbow spray as they plunged downwards. Carrying my worldly goods on my back, I walked down the long, winding road to the ferryboat station at the bottom. By the time I reached it I had decided the fjord was ideal for my purpose. So I took photographs, ate my packed lunch, and started back.

I soon found the miles up to the fjord were much longer than the miles down, particularly as it was a very hot day. High above me was an hotel, the Stalheim, sited to give a view down the spectacular fjord, and I made it my target. As the road grew steeper and the sun beat down, I began having visions of the cold beer I would enjoy when I reached it.

I haven't a record of the time it took me, although it must have been at least two hours. I was now stripped to the waist and my shorts were drenched in sweat. With my thirst prodigious, I was entering the hotel courtyard when a loud cheer stopped me in my tracks. Ahead of me was a party of American tourists. They had been monitoring my progress most of the afternoon through binoculars and as I neared the hotel they had prepared my welcome. On the top of a wall that faced the fjord was a row of glasses, each one containing frosted beer. At such moments how can anyone help but like Americans?

*Gudvangen Fjord, Norway. Used to set my target in 633 Squadron.*

I met many attractive and interesting people during my ten days stay but no one more so than Fredrik Kayser. Kayser was one of the gallant Norwegian commandos who had destroyed the heavy water produced by and stored in the Norsk Hydro Power Station at Vemork, and possibly prevented Germany from winning the race for the atomic bomb. He was one of the two men who had entered the basement and blown up the storage tanks with plastic explosives.

He was now a councillor in Bergen and my reviewer friend, Eiliv, introduced us. Kayser's story of the raid and its perils fascinated me and I asked if he would give it to me in detail. He promised to do this but asked if I could return later in the year as his work load was heavy at that time. Feeling it was a story I must cover, I promised I would try.

On my return home I discovered letters from South Africa awaiting me. All were about *Laws* and all were unsigned. Three promised me that if I ever returned to the country I would not live a week. Others, although not quite so threatening, suggested my life would not be a happy one if I ever came back. From memory, one was on Parliamentary notepaper, which led to all kinds of imaginings. I had no idea how their authors had received copies because book sales were non existent in the Union. Whether this was because bookshops were afraid to stock the book or whether it came under the banned book list, I never found out. However, I did learn from friends that the book was available in the Union Castle ships that at the time plied to and fro from Southampton to Cape Town.

With Shelagh's relatives still in the Union, it meant I might have problems in accompanying her if any need arose for her return. At the same time I cannot deny there was satisfaction in knowing the book and its attack on apartheid had found their target.

## TWENTY-NINE

Before returning to Norway I contacted The Daily Express, who was featuring such articles at the time, to tell them of Kayser's offer. Would they be interested in the exclusive story, and if so, would they subsidize my trip?

They were very wary. They could not advance me more than £50 at this stage and their acceptance of the story and the price they would pay for it would be decided when it was written.

I talked it over with Shelagh, and although it meant I would be away for Christmas, we both decided it would be worth my going. I felt confident I could write a publishable article and I also felt the knowledge I would gain would be useful for future work, which proved to be true.

So early in December I crossed the North Sea again. I found Bergen a very different place from the city of the summer. The weather was changing almost daily from rain to frost and then rain again, and the pavements were slippery with rutted ice. Yet, with fairy lights strung on trees everywhere, it looked very pretty and I found myself falling in love with the country.

However, once more money was my problem. After buying a return ticket, there was little left of my £50 advance and so I found a small hotel which agreed to accommodate me without meals. My plan was to eat as cheaply as possible, mostly on sandwiches made in my room.

Fredrik Kayser kept his word and visited me two or three evenings a week. He would arrive around 7 p.m. and leave around 8.30 p.m. His story was an absorbing one and I found myself full of admiration for the skill and courage the 'Gunnerside' party had shown. Kayser himself was a pleasant man who spoke excellent English and after I took notes for the first hour, we would reminisce about the war. He knew Britain well, having spent many months training with the Linge Movement (Norwegian freedom fighters) up in Scotland.

I was hoping to get the full story before Christmas so I could get back home but with Fredrik taking his family away for the holidays, this was too ambitious. I would have to await his return after the festivities.

I was resigned to a somewhat gloomy Christmas in my room when Eiliv and his wife Gerd invited me to stay at their house in Paradis. They too were going away for Christmas, but I was free to use the spare room during their absence, and Eiliv's father, who lived close by, would like me to spend Christmas Day with him and his family.

I was only too glad to accept. With money running out, I was down to bread and goat's milk cheese, and if I could save on accommodation during the Christmas week, I might just be able to last out until I had the complete story.

Eiliv's spare room was in the basement and heated by an electric fire. As winter had now arrived with a vengeance and the snow-covered roads were hard with frost, I was told I must keep the heater on all night if the cold lasted. Then Eiliv and Gerd drove off.

They had thought of everything but not the heater breaking down. This happened on my second day and I hadn't the money to have it repaired. So I spent six of the coldest nights of my life wearing every stitch of clothing I possessed and huddled like an embryo in my duvet. I believe I was colder than in my days in Quetta.

Christmas came as a welcome break. Eiliv's father, a banker, lived in a house on the banks of the Nordensvannen, the lake overlooked by Edvard Grieg's home. Told to arrive early, I found myself having breakfast with his family and what a breakfast it was. Everyone seemed to be drinking aquavite, a drink which (for those innocents who have never encountered it) is also said to defrost windows, charge car batteries, and fuel rockets. In other words it is the most potent liquor I had ever tasted and yet everyone appeared to be drinking it neat.

This went on all day and yet no one seemed overly drunk. By this time I had already discovered that drinking was a Norwegian way of life. Perhaps the climate fostered it or perhaps it was the Scandinavian melancholy that needs it, but nowhere else in the world had I seen people who like drink more and yet remain so charming with it.

Be that as it may, by evening I was fit for anything. When I left around 1 am Eiliv's father wanted to drive me back to his son's house. When I refused his offer, he held out a cap with ear flaps. "You have quite a walk back to Eiliv's house and it is very cold tonight. If you do not cover your ears, they could be frostbitten."

I thanked him for his solicitude and for a happy day but still left the cap behind. With the moon floating like a silver coin over the hills and with the aquavite making me into a Nordic giant, I had no intention of returning home yet.

Instead I walked all round that beautiful frozen lake. The air was chilled wine, the moonlight shone down on the frosted trees, and a million diamonds shimmered and showered around me. My body had the strength of ten men and music from the spheres played from the enchanted sky. The glory of Grieg no longer awed me. I could have written Peer Gynt myself on that magical night.

I arrived back at my room around 3 a.m. and slept like a top until the sun rose. I decided aquavite suited my metabolism.

Fredrik arrived back before the New Year and completed the story in three more sittings. Before I left he gave me some photographs and then asked me for a promise. His comrades were still alive and neither he nor they wanted a highly-spiced English version of their epic action. Would I please keep strictly to the facts?

With the story so full of courage and hair-raising incidents, I had no hesitation whatever in making the promise. With that I thanked him, we said goodbye, and I took the next ship back to Newcastle.

As so often in my life, nothing was allowed to be that simple. During the night the ship began to pitch and roll as if she were a coracle and I was soon losing the dinner on which I'd spent the last of my Daily Express advance. It was the kind of storm that only shallow seas produce and just before dawn the ship shuddered and paused as if she had struck an undersea obstacle. The jerk was so violent that I was thrown headfirst from my bunk and half stunned as I hit a nearby bulkhead. Thinking the ship might be sinking, I staggered along a companionway to make enquiries of the crew. They took some finding because by this time many were sick themselves. Reassured that the ship wasn't too badly damaged, I returned to my bunk and retched away until sunrise.

On deck the following morning the damage was apparent. When I enquired about the huge jolt, I was told it had been caused by a giant wave that had ripped off one of the ship's stabilizers. My clearest memory of that morning, however, was the sight of a little girl carrying a bottle of aquavite across the Customs Shed when we eventually berthed. It was, I learned later, a present for her father. But the night had been too much for the child and as she neared a table, her wobbly legs gave way and the bottle crashed into splinters on the cement floor. It was a moment that made even the hard-bitten Customs officers leave their tables to dry her tears.

After checking all was well with the family, my first task on arriving home was to convert my notes into an article. I took great care over it and felt I had done a reasonable job when I posted it off to the Express.

I was quickly disappointed. I was told the article must have some female participation if it were to appeal to the newspaper's readers. It was also suggested that I should tighten up the suspense by using 'literary licence' here and there.

I found these suggestions absurd. The commandos had gone through experiences that even a feverish imagination would have found difficulty in matching. And how could I bring a woman into the operation without destroying its credibility? Moreover, I had obtained the story on the promise I would keep to the facts.

It was soon made clear to me that unless I sank my scruples the story would not be published and I would receive no further payment. Nor would I be likely to sell it as it stood or match their offer if I offered it elsewhere.

I can't deny I wasn't tempted. I was sick and tired of Shelagh always having to count the pennies. But I had made a promise to Kayser and it has always seemed to me that if a man foregoes his principles for profit, he is on the slippery slope to nowhere. So the answer had to be no and for a long time it seemed a considerable amount of time and work had been wasted. However I did eventually sell the story to a Commando Boy's Annual although the payment was small beside the Express earlier promise.

By the late summer of that year *633 Squadron* was finished and in the hands of Hutchinson. For myself I felt reasonably satisfied with it. I knew all my technical facts were accurate, I felt the characters were alive and true to life (after all, I had drawn many from men I had known), and I knew the air battles had total authenticity. In other words I liked to think that my late colleagues, for whom it was my small testament, would approve of it.

But not so Hutchinsons. To my surprise and dismay they said the story disappointed them. My first two novels had made them believe I was a young novelist with new things to say, but instead I had given them yet another war novel. War books, they said, had flooded the market during the last ten years and the public was sated by them (this in 1955!). They doubted if they would sell enough *633*s to pay for its publication. Nevertheless, in the hope that I would go on to write more original work, they had decided to support me by accepting the novel. But this decision could not allow me a greater advance than the one given for my previous novel.

This magnanimous gesture meant I was to receive £120 for another year's work. To say I was disappointed would be an understatement. I had never seen the story as purely a war novel. To me it was about the obscenity of war and its effect on young minds and their lives. That had been my purpose in writing it and it hurt to have it dismissed so glibly as 'yet another war novel'.

Not that others treated it so dismissively. A Canadian magazine bought the serial rights and the following year Hutchinson's Rights Manager told me, again with self-gratification, that he had 'persuaded' Emmet Dalton to buy a £200 film option on the story. If Dalton took up the option within a year he would pay a further £1,300. From this £200 I had to pay Hutchinson 25% commission.

This Dalton contract was never shown to me. Because Hutchinson had demanded control of the cinematography and television rights along with other rights in their original book contract, such deals were made without my knowledge of their details.

I cannot say the money was not welcome but again I had the feeling Hutchinson's cavalier approach to my work was doing me no favours. Yet with our endless need for a decent income I was not in a position to query my contracts.

I did make one enquiry, however. Having recently discovered that the United States were not at that time in the Berne convention and therefore books should be copyrighted in their Library of Congress if they weren't to be pirated and put without payment into the public domain, I wrote Hutchinson to ask if my three novels had received this essential coverage. I received a curt reply from the Foreign Rights Manager that such matters were standard practice and my novels had been given the same protection as all their other novels. To my future regret I believed this assurance.

With Hutchinson not liking war novels, I had to think of a theme for my fourth work that they might like. So after talking it over with Shelagh, I decided on a period novel with two disparate women as its main characters. One would be the elderly chatelaine of a large family estate, the other the young bride of her only son whom he has just brought to England. The story line would then contain the mother-in-law's dismay when she discovers her only son's wife cannot bear a child. If the elderly woman were given the necessary characteristics, it could be a psychological thriller.

In theme it could hardly have been more different from my 633 Squadron but no doubt that was in my mind. With Shelagh believing the story line had promise, I decided to go ahead and write it.

This I did and worked on it throughout the rest of that year and into 1956. But I must have worked too hard because quite suddenly I had an alarming breakdown in health. In the middle of one night, while asleep, I felt a sudden fierce pain in my chest and my heart stopped beating. In the nightmare that followed I was falling down a deep grey shaft with despairing voices calling at me from all sides. With all vital functions having ceased, it seemed life was over. Then, with a great thud, my heart began beating again but not in the accepted sense. It pounded and raced like an uncontrolled machine.

I awoke to find sweat not only soaking through my pajamas but soaking through the blankets as well.

With Shelagh afraid I had suffered a heart attack, she insisted I saw our doctor. To my surprise and relief he found nothing organically wrong with me and suggested I had suffered nothing more than a bad nightmare. Yet the very next night the same thing happened. The pain was intense and when my heart resumed beating its rate was nearly two hundred a minute.

The attacks continued and somehow I managed to continue working but I began to dread the nights. Eventually it was Shelagh who thought of my literary benefactor, Dr MacKay. He was a psychiatrist and if these attacks were not organic he might be able to help me. Agreeing, I phoned him with my problem.

He first gave me a full physical examination to confirm that my heart was sound. Then, after making enquiries about my life style, he gave thought to my problem. In his view I was paying the price for four years of unremitting mental work, with the additional problems of penury added to them. The resultant stress could have displayed itself in cramp, usually in the arms or legs. In my case, almost certainly because of the psychological scar inflicted on me by my doctors ten years earlier, it was making itself felt in my heart muscles.

In other words I was suffering from false angina. The attacks would not kill me but they might well continue for weeks or months ahead. MacKay suggested a long rest from work and also a holiday because, when the attacks were as severe as mine, they could eventually lead to a mental breakdown.

I remember well my thoughts when I left his surgery that day. In my desire to be a writer I had not only brought Shelagh from that paradise in South Africa but had also brought this damned infliction on myself. If one thing is certain in this life, it is that one pays a price for everything.

There was clearly no way I could take a long rest from work, but it did seem a break of some kind was necessary. After talking it over with Shelagh and having gained a liking for Scandanivia, I wrote the Swedish Tourist Board asking if they would employ me to write a series of travel articles for the British Press.

To my surprise they agreed to give me six weeks free travel on the Scandinavian Railways. Food and accommodation I would have to find for myself.

Shelagh, who could not accompany me because of the children, urged me to accept the offer and go. She also pointed out that if I could sell Scandinavian travel articles on my return, they would more than pay for the trip.

There was, however, the novel, which I called *Lydia Trendennis*, still to complete. So in spite of Dr. MacKay's protests and the recurring attacks, I managed to do this during the next few weeks.

I then approached a literary agency I had recently heard about. Although as yet I wasn't aware of the enormity of Hutchinson's neglect of my interests, I had realized that a good literary agent would handle my affairs better than I. At first I had thought of Laura Sagar but then discovered she specialized only in Scandinavia. So I hunted around and finally approached a company called The Literary Agency Management.

It proved to be a new company run by two men in late middle age, one named Ian Thompson and the other Reggie Turnor. They sent me a booklet to read and when it seemed satisfactory, I went to London to meet them.

Of the two men Reggie Turnor was the one I favoured. He was a tall, quietly-spoken man with the courtesy that often comes from a non-commercial background. I was further drawn to him when I learned he had published five novels of his own which surely meant he had an understanding of a novelist's problems. The result was I gave him two manuscript copies of *Lydia* to negotiate. Then, carrying my few needs in a haversack, I left for Scandinavia.

# THIRTY

My first stop was Copenhagen. Liking the city, I stayed there for three days in the Youth Hostel, then crossed the Kattegat to Helsingborg in Sweden. From there I took the train to Goteborg, then on to Stockholm.

By this time I was finding it one of the most fruitful journeys of my writing life. In every place visited I seemed to find someone compatible with whom I could share interests and experiences. No doubt this was made easier by my staying in youth hostels where the residents shared the kitchens and dormitories and so faced no communication barriers. I met Norwegians, Danes, Swedes, Germans, French, Americans: the list seemed endless and with them I must have walked dozens of miles in each city, taking in the sights and sounds. I also walked many more miles on my own in the country, trying to relax the tension that had built up within me during the previous four years.

I spent a week in Stockholm, where I stayed on the three-masted sailing ship used as a youth hostel. I then took the Nordic Express to Kiruna, which was well inside the Arctic Circle. This train journey was an experience in itself for although I left Stockholm in late August, when I drew back the curtains of my sleeper the following morning, the tundra was a splendour of red and gold as far as the eye could see. In twenty-four hours I had travelled from summer to autumn.

I had a couple of days in Kiruna, where I was lucky enough to be invited by a party of Americans to join their trip into the famous iron ore mountain. I then moved along the rail track to the famous Abisko National Park where migrant birds from China can be found. Fascinated by the blaze of colour everywhere, I spent over a week there, often walking twenty miles a day and more along the many quiet footpaths. Finally I borrowed heavy walking boots and a compass, crossed the great Tornetrask lake, entered Norway, and days later found myself somewhere along the Finnish border. By this time I had run out of food and had two more days of walking before finding the Abisko Centre again. I was as hungry as a wolf by this time but I felt wonderful. All the poisons of a modern, civilized life seemed to have sloughed from me and my false angina attacks, if not wholly cured, had become far less frequent.

All this travelling was done on a few krona. The Scandinavians, and particularly the Swedes, provided accommodation for all pockets: the Abisko Centre had seven grades, from en suite apartments down to dormitories. I used the latter and had no regrets. Lying at nights watching the huge Nordic moon floating over the silver Tornetrask, I envied no man his wealth or his status. My only wish was that I had Shelagh and the boys with me.

With regret I took the train back to Stockholm and spent a few days roaming about central Sweden. Unable to afford accommodation, but having a first class rail ticket, my ploy was to sleep in the trains at night and, by studying rail schedules, organize my journeys so as to arrive at a given destination by morning. Thus I might travel a thousand miles to cover one hundred. However, as first-class carriages were usually half-empty, I was cheating no one of his seat and the conductors offered no protests.

I arrived back in Stockholm and on collecting my mail I found an excited letter from Shelagh. My new agency had sold the first serial rights of *Lydia Trendennis* to the magazine Woman for £1000.

I had to sit down and take it in slowly. At that time Woman had the largest circulation of any similar magazine in England, in the region of six million. And they had taken my novel for serialization! This surely must be our breakthrough at last.

I sent a cable to Shelagh, telling her I'd received the news and was on my way home. Then, with a friend from the ship, I allowed myself a small celebration.

On my return home I was told by Camilla Shaw, the fiction editor of Woman, that *Lydia* would first appear on the 29th December. (In fact it was to be published under its original name of *The Second Lydia Trendennis*). It would be featured in six weekly instalments and would be the main fictional story of that period.

I was not asked to make this adaptation, nor did I mind. I felt, probably wisely, that shaping a novel to suit a magazine's

requirements was specialist work and I would be better employed in getting on with my next novel. This I intended to do as soon as I thought of a suitable plot. In the meantime I wrote travel articles about Sweden and had one of them published in the English newspaper The Guardian.

*633 Squadron* was published in October. Soon the reviews began to arrive and after Hutchinson's depressing forecasts their contents might be of interest. The Times Literary Supplement found it 'true to its background and genre — the fictional equivalent, one might say, of Terence Rattigan's *Flare Path*. Another reviewer, after praising its reality and technical accuracy, claimed it to be 'just about the best novel dealing with the RAF' that he had come across. But the most satisfying comment came from Douglas Bader, to whom I'd sent a signed copy soon after publication. His letter read:

*Dear Frederick Smith,*

*Some long time ago you sent me a book called 633 SQUADRON, and soon after you sent it I disappeared abroad for a fairly long session. I have just finished reading the book and so has my wife, and we both liked it enormously. I am not normally a reader of war books or prisoner of war books, and therefore when I pick one up and read it right through, you can rest assured that I am not by any means flattering you when I say it has to be good.*

*Many thanks for sending it to me, and good luck for any future books you may write. With kind regards, Yours sincerely,*

*Douglas Bader.*

No letter I have received before or since gave me more pleasure or satisfaction. I felt if I had convinced Bader of the authenticity of my novel, I need not worry too much about the opinions of men who had never known the stresses of squadron life and the tensions of aerial combat. It was not long before a second hardback edition was published and Arrow Books brought out a paperback. Modest though these sales were, they were the best I'd received to date. What I had no way of knowing at the time were the traumas and the triumphs this novel was to bring in the years ahead.

> 20th May 1957.
>
> Dear Frederic Smith,
>
> Some long time ago you sent me a book called 633 Squadron, and soon after you sent it I disappeared abroad for a fairly long session.
>
> I have just finished reading the book and so has my wife, and we both liked it enormously. I am normally not a reader of war books or prisoner of war books, and therefore when I pick one up and read it right through, you can rest assured that I am not by any means flattering you when I say it has got to be good.
>
> Many thanks for sending it to me, and good luck for any future books you may write.
>
> With kind regards,
> Yours sincerely,
>
> *[signed] Douglas Bader*
>
> Frederic Smith Esq.,
> 5 Spinney Walk,
> Anlaby Park,
> HULL, YORKS.

*Copy of Douglas Bader's original letter*

There was further good news about *Lydia* just before Christmas, when Shelagh and I were being entertained by two Danes, Vigo and Greda Jensen, who lived near to Mr England's house. We had met them through our respective children, who went to the same school, and had become good friends. Vigo was an international footballer who had won a soccer bronze medal at the Olympic Games two years earlier and was now playing for the Hull City football team. As my work was sedentary and I felt it necessary to compensate by getting plenty of physical exercise, he sometimes arranged for me to attend his team's training sessions.

This particular afternoon we were watching a sports programme on their television - a treat for us who owned no such luxury at that time - when the door bell rang. Vigo went out and returned with a telegram which he handed to me. It seemed Mr England, who knew where we were spending the afternoon, had sent the messenger over to us. Puzzled, for I seldom received telegrams, I tore it open to read the cryptic message: PHONE ME AT OFFICE. URGENT. REGGIE.

We had no telephone but Vigo insisted I used his. Wondering what had happened and full of excitement, I got through to the office, only for a typist to tell me Reggie had slipped out for a few minutes but would phone me on his return.

Unable to find out anything more from the typist, I had to bite my nails for another ten minutes before the phone rang. It was Reggie and he sounded excited. The Rank Organisation were offering £2000 for the film rights in *Lydia*. They had contacted him just before lunch. Would I accept their offer?

Would I? I stammered out my acceptance and then ran back into the sitting room to tell Shelagh. I think we did a jig around the settee. *Lydia* was doing wonderful things for us. We were now safe for another year. For eighteen months even, if we were careful. As delighted as we were, Vigo and Greda joined us in a heartfelt celebration.

So it was a good Christmas that year. After four bleak years it was a huge relief to afford presents and the little luxuries that go with the season. With Shelagh's Dad still with us, we spent the day with my parents and Ray who had come up from London for the holidays. They must all have been as relieved as we were at our change of fortune, and after dinner we taped a message for Shelagh's mother in South Africa. Later in the month I bought a small cine camera in order to send her moving pictures of our children growing up. In all ways it was a Christmas to remember.

There was also the first exposure of *Lydia* to anticipate, although at times I had misgivings of this. *Lydia* was an experimental novel for me and as it was being featured under my real name, I wondered if women would accept the story on seeing it was written by a man.

I need not have worried. As a serial *Lydia* was unquestionably a success. After the last instalment appeared, Camilla Shaw wrote to tell me she had received hundreds of letters praising it and that the sales of Woman during the six weeks of publication had risen by an average of 96,000. If I wished to write any more in the same vein she would be more than interested. When the French magazine Marie Claire bought the serial rights, I realized I had struck a rich vein. If I could write a story matching *Lydia* I would have the largest and most profitable publishing market in Britain open to me.

But that meant conceiving another story like *Lydia*. At first it seemed merely a matter of time, but as the first buds appeared on the crab apple tree below my attic, I began to wonder if *Lydia* had been a one-off story and I would never think of another like it.

Believing that women like stories about children, I finally decided to write one about an orphan girl who had been adopted for the wrong reasons by selfish parents and suffered accordingly.

But first I moved office. Although my night attacks were not so frequent after my Scandinavian trip, I was still having one occasionally, and my good friend John MacKay felt an escape from that claustrophobic attic would be beneficial. So I asked my parents if I might use their spare room during the daytime. When they agreed, I moved my typewriter and equipment there and made the journey every day as if I were a clerk going out to work.

As the distance was only a mile or two, I found myself enjoying the daily walks and wished I had thought of it earlier. I was less happy with the new novel, however. Although I liked the story as it was developing, the uncomfortable feeling grew on me that for a popular magazine I was digging too deeply into the psychology of the situation and not giving enough time to any necessary romantic aspects. I kept trying to lighten the pages but then felt I was doing the very thing my incensed Collett's manager had wrongly accused me of: by treating a serious subject too flippantly.

Such conflicting thoughts taught me things both about myself and my profession. *Lydia* had started off as a psychological study of a sick and obsessed woman, but somewhere along the line — almost certainly because the theme had permitted it — it had drifted off into a thriller. In doing so I had missed the stars at which I'd so ambitiously aimed, but instead had written a story perfectly suited for magazine readers.

I could not help contrasting *Lydia* with *Laws*. In *Laws*, trying to create real characters in real situations, I had spent over two years and even risked my life during them, and what had my return been — £120. Even *633 Squadron* for all its fact, colour and nostalgia, had not yet done as well for me as this single Cornish thriller.

It all seems naive today but this was the first time I had faced the choice confronting me. If I decided to write thrillers — and I had proved that I could write them — then there was every chance I could make real money and give Shelagh the life she deserved. But if I chose serious themes, then in all likelihood we would remain relatively poor for the rest of my writing life.

I hadn't thought in these terms before because until then my main ambition had been to appear in print. But now the choice was there. I knew well enough my own predilections. I had always admired the French penchant of using fiction as a medium of influence because everything I had learned in life had taught me that a man's views are seldom changed by direct argument. When an attack is expected his defences are prepared. But emotions cannot be so easily controlled, and if a novel is cleverly written, his prejudices can often be breached before he knows they are under attack.

This had always seemed to me the great potential of the novel and the one I wanted above all else to exploit. But I had Shelagh and the children to consider and it only seemed right that she who had endured so much for me, should give her opinion.

Looking back I knew her views before I asked for them. I must write what I wanted to write and it would all work out in the end, she told me. When a man lives with such a woman, even the worst of us are moved to compromise. So I made the private decision to write one serious novel and then one popular one until our security was established. In making this decision, I made myself one promise. No matter how long I had to write popular books, I would never treat them with contempt. Within their limitations, I would always give them the best writing and construction of which I was capable. In this way I would be able to display them on my bookshelves without shame or embarrassment.

I remember one disturbing thought emerging from all this mental conflict. If successful cliché-ridden blockbusters needed no purpose in their structure except to entertain, then were not authors with meretricious minds the luckiest among us? Probably because I wasn't certain where I stood myself, I pushed the thought away and applied my new concepts to the adopted child novel.

I soon realised I was trying to marry two incompatibles. On the one hand I was trying to write a popular magazine story and on the other to demonstrate the harm that loveless parents could inflict on a child's mind. Feeling the subject was unsuited for the former, I opted for the latter and interviewed people from every profession dealing with children to gain their viewpoints and opinions. Armed with all this information, and with the romantic aspect of the novel no longer inhibiting me, I plunged into it with new enthusiasm. For better or worse the die with this novel was cast.

# THIRTY-ONE

While I was busy writing the novel, which I had already entitled *The Sin and the Sinners*, Reggie Turnor continued to market *Lydia* and soon sold both the Norwegian and the Italian serial rights. The monies for these sales were only small but they were all bonuses and I congratulated myself in taking on an agent. Reggie Turnor was equally enthusiastic, particularly when I learned later that the sale to Woman was the first sale the new agency had made.

As a book, *Lydia* was scheduled for publication later in the year and I was wondering what promotion and advertising Hutchinson intended for it. Whatever its literary merits, I knew from the hundreds of letters received by Woman, some of which were sent to me, that many readers wanted to buy the novel either for themselves or as gifts to others, and so wanted to know the date of publication. But here was the rub. Until now my novels had been advertised in the so-called quality newspapers, like The Times, The Observer, and The Daily Telegraph. Although this suggested the books were deserving of their niche, I was already blasé enough to know the second reason. It was far cheaper to advertise in these newspapers than in the tabloids whose sales ran into millions.

I had raised no objection regarding my three earlier novels (a) because I hadn't dared to, and (b) because I had felt, rightly or wrongly, that a reader of the Observer might find their subjects more to his liking than a reader of the tabloids.

But *Lydia* was different because of its theme and story line. Its advertisement in the quality newspapers would at the best result in only a few thousand sales but advertising in the magazine that had first featured it could be very profitable, particularly when readers were asking for its publication date.

So I felt justified in suggesting to Hutchinson that instead of its advertising budget going into the quality newspapers, it might be better spent on one single but striking advertisement in Woman.

My suggestion was treated with the tolerance reserved for young writers who have yet to understand the whys and wherefores of the world. I was told my suggestion was noted but it was not house policy to advertise in the mass media.

I could not accept that. I felt it was far more sensible to alert people who liked its kind of story and particularly those who had read it and now wanted to buy it. So I requested an interview with the Company Chairman, Robert Lusty. Lusty was said to be the highest paid publisher in London at that time and the size of his office seemed to confirm it. Determined not to be over-awed, I put my case to him.

His answer was that a young novelist could not expect a promotion budget large enough to cover an advertisement in a popular magazine. Nor had it any point because time had shown that such readers did not buy books. In any case, company policy was to advertise only in the 'better press.' The sonorous pronouncements rolled out like lessons from Moses. No matter that I told him about Woman's huge increase in circulation, the hundreds of letters that had been sent them, that if only one percent of Woman's readers bought the novel it would mean sales of at least 60,000. My mathematics only received a paternal smile and the comment that such matters were irrelevant in any case because it had long been proven that only word of mouth sold books and so advertisements only served to keep a company's imprint before the public eye. With that a secretary was called and my interview was over.

*Lydia* was published on the 24th of July. It was advertised in the Times, the Observer, and The Daily Telegraph. Its final sales when the figure was finalized were less than 5,000! Not for the first or the last time in my life I wondered if publishers really wanted to sell books.

Nevertheless *Lydia* gained many reviews and because of my earlier thoughts about story lines I read them with interest. Although some critics labelled it a melodrama, which I fully accepted, almost all praised its construction. Books and Bookmen said it was a good enough piece of writing to keep a reader engrossed from the first page to the last. Books Of The Month said it was an exciting tale guaranteed to thrill and was packed with surprises and dramatic situations; and Vanity Fair called it a first rate thriller and quite truly a book that 'you can't put down'. As for the professional magazine The Writer, it flattered me by saying 'Frederick E. Smith has an outstanding gift — he can tell a story. The construction of *Lydia* is faultless.'

I was both surprised and pleased by these opinions although more than one review suggested there were shades of Daphne Du Maurier and *Rebecca* in the story. This assumption was quite wrong. I had never read a word of *Rebecca* when conceiving the story nor when writing it.

I bought a car that year for £450, a second-hand Hillman Husky. It was my first car, and as I had never learned to drive, my father took Shelagh and I out in the evenings to give us driving lessons. I took my driving test in August, failed it the first time by going down a one-way street, but passed on the second attempt. I then suggested to Shelagh that we took it over to Europe the following year. 1958 was to be the year of the huge Brussels Exposition and my plan was to drive around France and Germany for a fortnight and then complete the holiday by spending a day at the Exposition. Bravely Shelagh agreed and we began making plans.

*633 Squadron* came into life again in June when I received a letter from Hutchinsons telling me that Emmet Dalton had taken up his film option on the book and had forwarded them the balance of the option, which was £1,300. My share, £975, would be sent to me in due course.

Although the payment seemed very small after the reviews received, I had no option but to accept. It proved to be my total payment for the film sale. Had I known at the time what triumphs and traumas would come from this sale, I would probably have cut my throat. But both were hidden in the future.

Although *The Sin and the Sinners* was more or less completed by the end of 1957, I spent another month honing and polishing its first few chapters before I took a deep breath and asked Reggie Turnor to send it to Woman.

I had my reply within a few weeks. Woman liked the story very much but sadly didn't feel the subject suitable for their wide readership. However, their interest in me remained strong and they hoped I would let them see my next work.

I cannot say I was surprised. I had already learned there is a price to pay for one's views and beliefs. At the same time if no one but Hutchinsons were to take it, and that was by no means certain, we would be getting a poor return for a year's work.

So it proved. After nearly six weeks Hutchinson told us they had decided to publish the book through Jarrolds, one of their subsidiary companies. If this were acceptable, Jarrolds would advance £90 on signing the contract and a further £90 on publication. As Reggie Turnor didn't feel I would do any worse under this new imprint, I had little choice but to take his advice and agree the terms. At the same time I was puzzled because Raymond Anderson had told me he wanted more novels from me like *Laws* and *Masks* and I felt *The Sin* was as good as either. Then I discovered Anderson had left the firm and wondered if that was the explanation for these recent changes.

However, the disappointment had one positive effect. As it seemed *The Sin* would not tap the profitable magazine market, this was surely the time to put my decision into practice and write a 'popular' novel. Although in our modest terms our bank balance was relatively sound at the moment, with two children growing up fast, we knew we could easily be back in financial difficulties the following year.

In part this was because we had decided to buy a house with the proceeds from *Lydia*'s film sale. We knew it was a gamble but had we not been gambling for the last five years? So while we began searching for a house within our means, I decided to make my next book a thriller, the kind that would hopefully appeal to both men and women. Indeed it would need to have such an appeal if we were going to invest nearly all our capital in bricks and mortar. So while we consulted building societies and went through the rest of the hassle that moving house entails, I tried to work out a promising story line.

I have never been certain what made us decide to leave Hull and move south, particularly when most of our friends lived there. Perhaps it had something to do with the weather. Mr England's house was built like so many northern houses of its period with totally inadequate insulation. As a result cisterns invariably froze in inclement weather, which left a tenant two choices before going to bed. He could either go into the street, open up the stop cock cover, plunge his hand to the elbow in icy water, turn off the house water supply and then drain the house system, or he could funk the operation, only to find the upstairs water tank frozen solid the next morning. In the latter case this meant heaving oneself bodily up through a tiny trapdoor in the bathroom ceiling and getting one's wife to hand up buckets of hot water. A man's courage on the day decided which choice was made.

It has also to be said that Mr England's habits did nothing to improve matters. Like many other countrymen of his time, his living room was his kitchen and although he would stoke up his coal fire and sit before it, he would also leave open the door that led out into the garden. He would do this even when force ten gales were blowing, with the result a knife-like draught would sweep beneath our sitting room door and neatly chop off the feet of anyone sitting near it.

We tried every way possible to change this habit. Didn't he realize he was no longer a young man and taking terrible risks with his health? Didn't he realize that one day he would catch pneumonia and die? His reply would be a little chuckle. He? Die from fresh air? It was the fresh air that kept him hale and hearty.

Then didn't he realize that the draught was causing amputations in our sitting room? Another chuckle at the softness of our generation. Fresh air was good for us, particularly for the young lads. They'd grow up with constitutions like his own. But if we really felt the cold that much, then why didn't we stuff strips of newspaper beneath the door? That would keep draughts out. We tried and in seconds sheets of newspaper were flying around the room like windswept seagulls.

But we loved the old man and so there were other reasons for

our move. One was the distance from London. Now that I had an agent, it was to my advantage to see him from time to time, and the train service from Hull took four and a half hours. Travelling by car was equally difficult with the so-called Great North Road little more than twenty feet wide in stretches. On top of this was the expense of each journey.

But, looking back, it was perhaps the North's attitude to art and literature that was the biggest factor. I can truthfully say I had no great wish for personal renown, which I've always felt to be a handicap rather than an asset, but regrettably a writer's name is his trademark and if it is suppressed, he will not progress. Whenever I had reason to mention my work to anyone other than the media, I would be faced with a sudden silence or a swift change of conversation to another subject. It gave one the feeling one was engaged in a disreputable profession, like selling dirty postcards, and that one ought to pull oneself together and do a decent job like being a postman or a second hand car salesman.

This odd attitude towards the arts showed itself in a hundred small but significant ways. Although I was the only working novelist in Hull at that time, I was never invited to join or even to attend any of its literary societies. It seemed fit and proper to recollect and even to acclaim dead authors and equally proper to stamp down firmly on current, local upstarts. Even when my old headmaster offered my school library some of my published books they were never put on to the shelves. At times one wondered whether a successful bank robber would have carried more scholastic pride than a shameful career in letters. At least it would have been more macho.

It was all petty, nit-picking stuff and as such should not have bothered me, particularly as I have an affinity to the North and like the friendliness of its people. In fact if I had not heard of other Northern writers with similar experiences I might have believed myself going through a period of paranoia.

Certainly Shelagh had no part in my restlessness. In spite of our earlier privations she had always seemed happy there and she liked all my friends. But it was the first time we had possessed enough money to think of buying a house and I knew the chance might not come again. So taking everything into account we finally opted to take the step, although exactly where was still undecided.

It was during this time that I met an editor who was to become a lifelong friend. A letter arrived one day from the Fiction Editor of Thomson-Leng Publications, asking if he might visit me. If I would give him a date, he felt it would be to my advantage.

A date was duly fixed and I met David Doig at Paragon Station. He was a sparse Scot with a small military moustache and a Dundee accent. On our way home he told me that he had read *Lydia* in Woman and had found it the ideal serial for one of his own magazines. He had come to see if I would sell him the 2nd British Serial Rights.

Although I couldn't make the sale without first phoning Reggie Turnor, this proved no obstacle. If Doig approached him, the two of them would agree on terms. I told this to Doig and we spent the rest of the afternoon getting to know one another. He was an affable man and Shelagh and I found we shared many interests. I think we were already friends before his train left for Dundee that evening.

I have forgotten what I eventually received for these 2nd serial rights but it can't have been much less than two hundred pounds. Once again *Lydia* had come up trumps and I must have felt some regret that *The Sin* was not following in its footsteps. Reggie was trying it on magazine after magazine but although editors kept praising it as a novel, they all said it was too serious a story for their readership. With our house purchase in mind, I was now convinced I must make my next novel a thriller. As yet I had not worked out a story line but with the accommodation matters taking up so much of our time I decided that for once my writing would have to wait until all the unsettling problems were resolved.

## THIRTY-TWO

There is no doubt that London should have been my aim when moving house. Everything I have seen since convinces me that writers who live there have an enormous advantage over the rest of us. As in almost any other profession, the people one knows are more important than the talent one possesses, and London life with its clubs, literary parties and junkets provides a rich environment for an ambitious scribe. It also housed the majority of publishers and agents.

But we had two small children to think about and London did not seem the place in which to rear them. Moreover, Shelagh was not the sort of woman who would enjoy buttering up agents, publishers and producers, and I was hardly cut out for the exercise myself. It had always seemed to me that in a true democracy a man ought to succeed on his talent alone and if he does not, then his society is guilty of prejudice and bias. It is, of course, a very old-fashioned philosophy — perhaps it has always been an old-fashioned philosophy — but a man has to live by his beliefs and if they hinder his progress, then so be it.

We finally decided a south coast town would suit us. Shelagh had grown up by the sea and I had developed a taste for it myself during my time in South Africa. Moreover it would be relatively close to London for any necessary visits,

But which town? So in the summer, leaving the children with my parents, we drove down to Brighton. Being only sixty miles from London, it seemed a likely place for a writer.

It was but not for this one. Shelagh and I had already decided that when we moved we were taking my parents with us. Both were now past retirement age but were having to continue working to meet the mortgage payments on their house. To leave them behind after all they had done for us, to take away the grandchildren they had looked after so often, seemed out of the question.

But it did mean our taking out a mortgage on a large house and in a profession like mine it meant taking a huge, financial risk. Nevertheless Shelagh showed no hesitation. I remember thinking how blessed I was to have a wife who not only was prepared to accept such a risk but also to share a house with an older family. Appreciating what they had done for us, she was as keen as I that they should retire and enjoy a well-earned rest.

But rates proved a problem in Brighton. We found plenty of large and suitable houses but in every case the rates were too high. As rates seemed to diminish in adverse ratio to the distance from London, we found ourselves driving westwards until we reached Bournemouth.

We had both friends and relations there. My old school friend Stewart Cottingham was now married and working for Vickers at Hurn Airport. My Aunt Lena and her daughter and son-in-law were also now living in the town. So the prospects were auspicious even before we arrived there.

We spent a couple of days with Stewart while we visited estate agents, to discover that rates were the lowest we had yet encountered because of the tourist trade. Deciding Bournemouth was for us, we arranged with Stewart and Peggy, his wife, to return in a few weeks to conduct a proper search.

This we did during the school holidays, leaving Pop, who was still with us, with Mr England. We found plenty of suitable houses although most were beyond our means. But eventually we came across one only five minutes walk from the cliff top that seemed to satisfy all our needs. It had four bedrooms on the first floor and two large attic rooms above. This meant we could give my parents three rooms and still have plenty of space for ourselves. The price was £3,250. Afraid of incurring a heavy mortgage, we decided to put down £2,500, although it left us with dangerously little capital for survival. But after all our travels and travails, the prospect of owning our own home was a heady brew. Surely, we argued, we must have turned the corner by this time and my thriller was certain to do well. Blinding ourselves to caution, we asked a local solicitor to set the purchasing wheels into motion.

Returning to Hull, we told my parents about our find and suggested they put their house on the market. Here they were lucky. My school friend Frank Holland and his wife were wanting to move and they decided the Northfield Road house was just what they wanted.

Thus all seemed set fair and by January 1958 we felt confident enough to settle on a removal date. Accordingly my parents and I booked vans from a Hull removal firm, Frank Holland did the same, as did their house buyer and all the others down the line of purchasers.

Then it happened. Two days before the vans arrived, an urgent telegram arrived from the Bournemouth solicitor confessing he had made a mistake. The man with whom he had been dealing did not own the house but had only an option on it. The real owner lived in Devon and would need to be consulted before a sale could go through. We would have to cancel all arrangements in the meantime.

It was a mistake that could only have stemmed from inefficiency and for us it meant apologies to everyone right down the line with the hope that nobody would sue us for compensation. Fortunately no one did, but the generosity of all concerned did nothing to improve my already damaged opinion of the professional classes.

We eventually moved down on the 28th April 1958, we driving down in the Husky and my parents and Pop following by train. We left on a bleak Northern day and arrived in springtime, with the front garden of the house ablaze with blue aubrietia. It was the first time my parents had seen the house and their pleasure added much to our own.

We talked over the partitioning of the rooms and it was decided they should have the two rear rooms on the first floor and the larger rear attic for a bedroom. We took the ground floor and the two second-floor bedrooms, and the front attic, which Pop could use for the rest of his stay in England. A large rear room on the ground floor was a problem because there was no way we could afford to furnish it. Finally we decided to set it aside as a playroom for the children.

So we settled in and spent the next few days finding a school for the two boys and seeing what amenities lay around us. Here we were lucky because there was a small park only a hundred yards away, the River Stour was a mere mile down the hill, and Hengistbury

Head could be reached by car in ten minutes. Even the New Forest was only a short drive away. It seemed by good luck we had chosen a house with excellent amenities.

*House in Southbourne with camper van, 1958*

So, in spite of the risks we were taking, 1958 seemed full of promise. By this time I had met my new editor at Jarrolds, Cherry Kearton, who was a relation of the famous naturalist, and found him a man I could relate to. He told me he liked *The Sin* very much and had hopes it would do well. Shortly afterwards it was published, and although the sales were no more than I expected, the reviews were excellent and pleased Kearton. Reggie also succeeded in selling the book to Sweden, and the reviews it received there were equally good. Although I received no royalties other than my advances from the sales, I wasn't too worried because at that time I seemed to have so many other strings to my bow. Woman were still encouraging me to write for them and David Doig kept suggesting I wrote a serial for one of his magazines.

Although it was my intention to write my thriller first, these interests suggested some kind of security and so, intrigued by our new and attractive surroundings, we indulged ourselves for the first time since returning to England. Packed in the little Husky, the six of us explored the New Forest, toured the Purbeck Hills, and took longer trips to Longleat and Stourhead.

Looking back, the move seemed to have gone to our heads because, compared with our earlier years, it was a year of recklessness. In mid summer, urged on by my parents who offered to look after the children, Shelagh and I did our two-week continental trip in the Husky, visiting Paris, Strasbourg, the Neckar valley, Holland, and finally the Brussels exhibition.

Of course it was all done on a shoestring. We slept in the Husky on a lilo bed and cooked on a tiny meths stove. Our only extravagance was our entry fee into the Brussels exhibition towards the end of our fortnight.

Until then we had enjoyed perfect weather but this night the skies opened up. We left the Husky in the centre of an enormous park packed with cars and fought our way into the exhibition itself. From then on we spent the evening running through the wind and rain from pavilion to pavilion. When we finally returned to the Husky we were drenched to the skin and had to take off every stitch of clothing. Huddled in blankets, too tired to blow up the lilo bed, we managed to fall asleep across the front seats. When we awoke, stiff and aching, Shelagh peered out through a misted window and then turned to me. "Have you seen outside?"

I looked and gave a start. Of all the hundreds of cars that had packed the park the previous night, we were the only one left: a tiny island in an enormous sea of wet tarmac. We looked at one another and then burst out laughing. Without being sure why, we felt the absurdity of the situation was typical of our lives.

With the holiday madness over it was time for me to think about work again, although to be fair to myself I had been working on shorter items, such as the Gunnerside story for Samson Low's book. Now I had to get to grips with the thriller. Although as yet I hadn't a story line, I did have a setting. While roaming around Lapland in 1956 it had occurred to me that I'd never read a novel set up there. As a result I'd taken notes of various sites and places in case they might be useful later.

These I now read again, and as they recollected the countryside that had excited me so much, I felt convinced I could come up with a colourful thriller if I went back there. But to take such a long trip on pure speculation was something we couldn't afford, so I contacted the Swedish Railways again. This time I intended to drive up to Stockholm by car and so only required free travel from that city to Kiruna.

It was given to me without quibble, perhaps because of the travel articles I had published, although this time I made it clear my purpose was to explore the possibilities of a novel rather than write more articles.

Grateful to the Swedes, I made my arrangements with Shelagh and then made ready to leave. I had no time to waste because it was the middle of August which already meant early autumn in Lapland. Excited at the prospects of seeing 'The Witch North' again as it is often called, I said au revoir to all the family and then drove off. I hadn't the faintest idea at the time that I was driving straight towards a personal melodrama.

## THIRTY-THREE

I had no firm plans when I took the Husky over to France except that my ultimate goal was Lapland. By this time I had evolved a philosophy about travel. To plan one's itinerary in total detail is only to experience one's itinerary. But unless one has a specific subject to study, should one not allow fate to have a voice in the proceedings?

My analogy is a man stepping into a rowing boat on a tidal river. If he rows from Point A to Point M, that will be the sum total of his journey. But if he rows into the middle of the river and ships his oars, the current will then take him where it wills. He will drift into coves and creeks that he never knew existed. His boat might, speaking philosophically, even take him to his destiny.

If ever a precept worked for a man, it worked for me during that 1958 journey. Driving up through the Netherlands and across Denmark, I finally arrived in Sweden. Because the weather was fine and I had a few days in hand, I decided to take a look at the Baltic and followed a coast road eastwards. Finally I reached a small town called Ystad where I decided to spend the night in its Youth Hostel. It was then my personal melodrama began.

There were a number of young people staying in the hostel. Among them was an attractive German girl in her late twenties whom I shall call Anna, and her brother whom I shall call Carl. Carl, three or four years older than his sister, looked decidedly unwell. I also had the strong impression that both were very frightened, although of what I had no idea.

They both spoke good English, and curious about them I drew them into conversation. Neither gave anything away but the following morning Anna said she was going into the woods to collect some edibles and would I care to go along and help her.

Curious what she meant by edibles, I did as she asked and watched her fill two sacks with roots and vegetation from the large wood behind the hostel. I carried the sacks back for her and that night she cooked us all a meal that I thoroughly enjoyed. Bursting with curiosity now, I asked how she had acquired all this wood lore but neither she nor her brother would tell me.

It took me another twenty-four hours to win their confidence and even then I think it was only because of Hobson's choice. They wanted to meet the ferry boat that crossed from Grossenbrode in Germany to Gedser, which was a few miles along the coast, and having no car to reach Gedser, they asked if I would take them to the port.

I agreed but when we reached the quay Anna puzzled me by asking for the car to be parked where we could remain unseen but could still view the passengers leaving the ferry.

I did as she asked and could feel her tension as she watched the passengers disembark. From her relief when the last one came down the gangplank, I knew that the person or persons whose appearance they were both dreading had not yet arrived.

By this time I felt they owed me an explanation and over a drink in a nearby cafe they finally gave it to me. It seemed their family were Berliners and in 1945, when the Russians had been advancing on the city, their widowed mother had fled with them into the Black Forest where they had managed to survive until military order had been established in Berlin. It was during this time that the girl had learned her wood lore survival skills.

On their return, Carl, like many other Berliners, had gone into the black market to help his family survive. During this period he had become involved with a gang leader called Steiner who had turned from normal black market activities into the more profitable trade of kidnapping political refugees and selling them to the Russians.

Carl, slipping into this dirty traffic by default, had been brought face to face with its consequences one night when he, Steiner and a henchman were driving with a captured refugee towards the Russian frontier. Deep into the mountains a police car had latched on to them and given chase. Gaining a little ground, Steiner had halted the car and ordered Carl and the kidnapped man to get out. He had given Carl a loaded pistol and told him to shoot the prisoner so there would be no witness to the crime. He and his accomplice had then driven off, leaving the frightened young man with a stranger to kill.

Drawn away by Steiner, the police car had shot past the two frightened men. The captive, whom Steiner had called Kleinberg, begged Carl for his life, promising he would not go to the police if he were released. Instead he would try to reach Sweden where he had relatives.

His pleas were unnecessary. Incapable of murder, Carl had already decided the only way out was to inform on Steiner and put himself at the mercy of the law. He told the terrified captive that the two of them must report to the police at once and tell them everything. With the kidnapping and selling of political refugees a capital offence in Germany at that time, the evidence they both gave would almost certainly put Steiner away for life and might even lead to his execution.

Realizing he was safe, Kleinberg promised he would report to the police in the morning and then ran off. Unable to stop him, Carl wasted no time in going to the police himself. They took down his statements, arrested Steiner and his accomplice the next day, and waited for Kleinberg to come forward.

To Carl's dismay, he never came. Without his evidence the kidnapping charge against Steiner was fatally flawed. Now Steiner could be charged only on lesser crimes for which Carl could give evidence. Nevertheless they still ended in Steiner receiving a long prison sentence. For his part in turning state evidence, Carl received three years imprisonment. To his massive relief he was granted a different prison to the revengeful Steiner.

Incredible though the story sounded, I was held by Anna's description of the trial. "I shall never forget the day of the sentence. Carl had been in the witness box and as Steiner was brought forward, they passed one another on the floor of the court. As they came abreast, Steiner stopped and looked at Carl with those devil eyes of his. He said nothing, did nothing, but both I and Carl knew that at least one death sentence was passed that day."

During Carl's imprisonment, Anna had done a variety of jobs

until her brother had rejoined her. Then, certain Steiner would take his revenge one day, they had spent their spare time and their savings trying to locate Kleinberg whose evidence could start a re-trial and put Steiner safely behind bars again.

At times it had seemed a hopeless task and as the date of Steiner's release had drawn nearer it became a desperate one. So when a detective agency had managed to trace Kleinberg to Stockholm, they had dropped everything and made straight for Sweden.

However. they had no sooner arrived than Carl had been taken ill and they had been forced to stay in the Ysted hostel until his recovery. This enforced stay had not only eaten into their small savings but two days earlier they had read in a German newspaper that Steiner had been released. Being certain that while he was in jail his contacts would have informed him of their activities and that he would move heaven and earth to prevent them from meeting Kleinberg, they were now frantic to reach Stockholm before he followed them. It was at this very point that I had run into them.

It all sounded a little too melodramatic and coincidental for me, but the girl was attractive, her brother was clearly unwell, and when Anna said she was certain Steiner would arrive in Sweden at any moment and asked me wistfully if I would be passing near to Stockholm on my way north, I impulsively offered to give them a lift there.

The following day we started off. As I was doubtful about their story, I had little thought of danger until we began climbing into a mountainous stretch of country. It was then that Anna, who had kept glancing anxiously back, said she believed there was a car trailing us. When Carl began to voice the same fears, I drove somewhat impatiently off the road to hide the car. Returning on foot, we hid behind a clump of trees so that we could watch the traffic go past.

After a few minutes a large American car came into sight. When I saw Carl's face and heard Anna's gasp of fear, I realized they were telling the truth. The car was being driven by a huge man and as it shot past I saw there were at least three other men packed inside it.

Expressing confidence I no longer felt, I told them not to worry.

We were behind the gang now and so they were unlikely to pick us up. What I had forgotten (or probably didn't know at the time) was that bridges had to be crossed to enter Stockholm, and all the gang needed to do on realizing they had lost us, was put a man on each bridge.

To cut the story short, we managed to get into Stockholm safely and after considerable danger and difficulties found Kleinberg whom the couple needed so desperately. It turned out he had not gone to the police on the fateful night because he was wanted himself for some criminal act. However, as he was now in great danger from Steiner, he had no choice but to agree to go with Carl and Anna to the Swedish police. Leaving the three of them there, knowing they would be safe in the hands of the police while the German authorities were alerted, I looked around Stockholm for a garage that would look after my car for the next couple of weeks. I then took the train to Kiruna.

From there I drifted to the Abisko National Park which had impressed me so much on my previous visit. There I had another bizarre experience. It was now early September and although the Arctic days were sunny, the evenings and nights were very cold. One day, dressed only in a shirt and shorts, I went for a long walk along a path that lay beside the railway track that ran from Kiruna to Narvik. My intention was to take a train back to Abisko before the icy evening arrived.

This train, the only passenger train that travelled in the late afternoon, stopped at only a few isolated stations. My aim was to reach one of these stations some twenty kilometres from Abisko, and make my return from there. But after I had been walking for a couple of hours and heard the far off hoot of a freight train, I realised that somehow I had strayed from the path and lost myself. By the time I retraced my way back to the railway line, I knew that unless I covered the last ten kilometres to the station quickly, I would be stranded for the night in inadequate clothing.

So I began to run. With a high cliff on one side and a steep drop on the other, I had to run more or less on the railway sleepers. Moreover, a thing I had forgotten, were the railway tunnels. There was one every mile or two, and in those days, and perhaps today for all I know, they were claustrophobic affairs so tightly cut they seemed to lack man-holes along their sides. The first tunnel I ran into was so long that for a full thirty seconds I could see no light at its far end, and in the total darkness I kept running into the rocky sides and bruising myself.

However, I came out of this one safely enough and was halfway through the second when an alarming thought struck me. Although few passenger trains used the line, this was not the case of freight trains. Huge thousand ton monsters packed with iron ore, left Kiruna every hour for Narvik. When had the last one passed by? Certainly not while I had been running along the track!

It took me no time to calculate that one was due at any moment and the tunnel I was in seemed endless. The faster I ran in the darkness, the more I stumbled over the sleepers or ran into the wet walls. Now and then I was forced to stop for breath and the pounding in my ears sounded like the pistons of an approaching train. Feeling one would be roaring down on me at any moment, I had no option but to continue running.

Daylight had never been more welcome than when at last I stumbled out of that tunnel and threw myself down alongside the track. As I fought for breath, a massive freight train burst out and thundered past me. I believe I had escaped death by no more than fifteen seconds.

When I recovered, I ran the remaining kilometres to the station where I was in time to catch the passenger train back to Abisko. By that time the writer in me had taken over and I was excited by my near escape. Until it had happened I had already worked out ways I could use my German girl and her brother in a thriller, but as yet had not thought of a satisfactory climax and ending. Now the tunnel incident had provided me with exactly what I wanted.

Two weeks later I returned home with almost a complete novel in my head. All because I had made no plans for my trip and simply 'followed my nose'. Moreover I now had a title for it too. It was *The Devil Behind Me.*

**Continued in Volume 3: The Final Absurdity**

Other titles by Frederick E. Smith curently available:

## A YOUTHFUL ABSURDITY
### An autobiography: Volume 1
### Pb. £10.50 inc.p&p  Hb. £16.50 inc.p&p (was £25)

In the author's own words:
"... Because this book covers my earlier years and because my age fated me to serve throughout the second world war, some of these events took place during that conflict.

"But ... it covers in the main the painful, the bizarre, and the often downright absurd events that plagued me from birth up to my twenty-sixth year...."

............................................................................................................

## THE FINAL ABSURDITY
### An autobiography: Volume 3
### (Provisionsl publication date: November 2012)

The final volume in this riveting autobiography of the writer's life continues to enthral. A fighter who believes in peace, a peacemaker who confronts bullies, a man of quiet courage and a steely determination to retain his independence and integrity as a full-time writer, whatever the frowns of fortune, never loses his sense of humour or fighting spirit.

............................................................................................................

## THE MYSTERIOUS AFFAIR
*Frederick E. Smith* £8.95 each (inc.p&p)

**THE MYSTERIOUS AFFAIR** is a gripping story about the strange liaison between RAF Flight Lieutenant Sean Hammond, DFC, a fighter-pilot and confirmed atheist who volunteers in 1939 because his hatred of bullies outweighs his distrust of patriotism, and Linda Martin, a devoted and married Christian with a deep, patriotic love of her country.

Inexplicably drawn to one another by forces beyond their control, they are totally unaware of the massive difference their chance meeting is to make on both themselves and the world around them.

# ORDER FORM

## Other Titles by Frederick E. Smith

*(All prices include post and packing)*

| Qty. | Title | Unit Price £ | Total £ |
|---|---|---|---|
| ........ | *The Mysterious Affair* | £8.95 | .................... |
| ........ | *A Youthful Absurdity (Vol 1:* pb) | £10.50 | .................... |
| ........ | *A Youthful Absurdity (Vol 1*: hb) | £16.50 | .................... |
| ........ | *An Author's Absurdities (Vol 2:* pb) | £9.50 | .................... |
| | | **TOTAL £** | |

Please send your order with cheque/postal order made payable to: **Emissary Publishing** at PO Box 33, Bicester, OX26 2BU.
*(Add £2.50 per book for Overseas Surface Post/Packing; ensure cheque is for sterling and drawn on an English Clearing Bank).*

Name..........................................................................................................

Address......................................................................................................

....................................................................................................................

....................................................................................................................

.................................................Post Code...............................

Date................................................................................................

Tel (in case of query)..................................................................

# EASY EXERCISES FOR THE OLDER PERSON
## by
### Monica P. File, MCSP
*(Cover design and illustrations by William T. File)*

**only £5.50 inc. p.&p.**

This book is intended for older people and carers.

It is easy to read and understand, giving beneficial exercises and general tips designed to help older or disabled people to maintain their health and independence.

The author is a chartered physiotherapist with forty years experience.

---

I wish to order_____copy/copies of *Easy Exercises For The Older Person* by Monica P. File, MCSP at £5.50 each (inc.p.&p.)

*(Add £1.00 per book for Overseas Post/Packing; ensure cheque is for sterling and drawn on an English Clearing Bank.)*

Please make cheque/postal order payable to:Emissary Publishing

Total amount enclosed:£_____Date_____

NAME (Block Capitals)_____
ADDRESS(Block Capitals)_____
_____
_____Postcode_____
Tel No. (if poss: in case of query)_____

**Please complete coupon and send with your cheque/postal order to: Emissary Publishing, P.O. Box 33, Bicester, Oxon, OX26 2BU, U.K.**